Unity 2D Game Development

Combine classic 2D with today's technology to build great games with Unity's latest 2D tools

Dave Calabrese

PUBLISHING

BIRMINGHAM - MUMBAI

Unity 2D Game Development

First published: March 2014

Production Reference: 1110314

Published by Packt Publishing Ltd.
Livery Place
35 Livery Street
Birmingham B3 2PB, UK.

ISBN 978-1-84969-256-4

www.packtpub.com

Cover Image by Dave Calabrese (dave@ceruleangames.com)

Credits

Author

Dave Calabrese

Reviewers

Greg Copeland

Fırtına Özbalıkçı

Karin Rindevall

Jack O. Snowden

Acquisition Editor

Rebecca Pedley

Content Development Editor

Sruthi Kutty

Technical Editors

Akashdeep Kundu

Neha Mankare

Faisal Siddiqui

Copy Editors

Roshni Banerjee

Mradula Hegde

Project Coordinator

Mary Alex

Proofreader

Paul Hindle

Indexer

Tejal Soni

Production Coordinator

Sushma Redkar

Cover Work

Sushma Redkar

About the Author

Dave Calabrese is an independent professional video game developer who has worked in the industry since 2002. Starting as an intern and working his way up to running his own small studio, Cerulean Games, he strives to produce fun and quality entertainment while also inviting others to learn from his experience and mistakes. Dave has had the opportunity to work on branded projects for top names and produce titles for multiple platforms, including Xbox 360, iOS, PC, and Mac. Today, he continues to produce fun and original games, participate in game jams, and author books.

Special thanks to my fiancée Kelly Myers for always putting up with my shenanigans.

About the Reviewers

Fırtına Özbalıkçı is an enthusiast of video games and game development tools. He is experienced in various game engines, including the Unreal Development Kit, Source Engine, Ogre3D, and Unity 3D. Additionally, he has studied open source physics engines such as Box2D in order to achieve a greater understanding of game mechanics. He has published several game mods and trainers and is a long-term contributor to several game development communities and GitHub. His latest project is a plugin to enhance the usability of the 2D physics of the Unity3D engine.

Fırtına is currently employed by a British billing company as a core developer. Previously, he worked for a visual effects company, specializing in production tools development. He graduated from the University of Bath in the United Kingdom, earning a degree with honors in Computer Science. He maintains a tiny garden in his London flat's balcony.

> I would like to thank my parents: Sonay and Erdoğan Özbalıkçı, my sister Goncagül, as well as Chelsea for their support in me being a reviewer.

Karin Rindevall is a Swedish animator and game artist with six years of experience in the gaming industry. She has worked with the Unity engine on several games released on various platforms. Her first Unity 3D title was MilMo (2008), the first 3D action adventure MMO played on a web browser. Today, she makes animation and art assets for 2D and 3D games released on PC and mobile devices at Hello There, a game studio in Gothenburg, Sweden. Their most recent game titles are Avicii | Gravity and Khaba. When Karin isn't creating games, she runs half marathons and creates comics.

Jack O. Snowden presently works for Wargaming of America, researching best practices for game development and game design. This includes environment design and modeling, texturing, object modeling, and game design.

He has worked at Electronic Arts Canada, Edmark (Riverdeep), spent a long extended time with Nintendo Software Technology, and finally as an academic director at the Seattle Art Institute, where he ran the gaming and animation departments.

www.PacktPub.com

Support files, eBooks, discount offers and more

You might want to visit www.PacktPub.com for support files and downloads related to your book.

Did you know that Packt offers eBook versions of every book published, with PDF and ePub files available? You can upgrade to the eBook version at www.PacktPub.com and as a print book customer, you are entitled to a discount on the eBook copy. Get in touch with us at service@packtpub.com for more details.

At www.PacktPub.com, you can also read a collection of free technical articles, sign up for a range of free newsletters and receive exclusive discounts and offers on Packt books and eBooks.

http://PacktLib.PacktPub.com

Do you need instant solutions to your IT questions? PacktLib is Packt's online digital book library. Here, you can access, read and search across Packt's entire library of books.

Why Subscribe?

- Fully searchable across every book published by Packt
- Copy and paste, print and bookmark content
- On demand and accessible via web browser

Free Access for Packt account holders

If you have an account with Packt at www.PacktPub.com, you can use this to access PacktLib today and view nine entirely free books. Simply use your login credentials for immediate access.

Table of Contents

Preface

Howdy and welcome! Take a seat and grab a drink. There you go. So, you say you want to learn all about this old-fashioned 2D stuff in that new-fangled Unity game engine? Well, you've come to the right place. Er, book. This here book? It's all about using those awesome 2D updates that Unity added in v4.3 to make an entire game. Yup, a whole, basic platformer, complete with parallax scrolling, enemy logic, UI, and a boss battle. Pretty sweet deal, eh?

What this book covers

Chapter 1, *Introduction to the 2D World of Unity*, covers the basics of getting Unity up and running for 2D games and setting up a simple, animated, sprite-based player character.

Chapter 2, *It Lives!*, is all about camera control, 2D triggers, player death and resurrection, firing a weapon, and a bit about state machines for good measure.

Chapter 3, *No Longer Alone*, adds enemies! Shoot them, get killed by them, and watch them patrol. It's a party where everyone wants to kill you!

Chapter 4, *Give It Some Sugar*, shows you how to build dynamic, endless enemy generation and a bigger game world, introduces parallax scrolling, and adds a scoring system.

Chapter 5, *The Ultimate Battle of Ultimate Destiny*, lets you know that the enemies have a friend, and he's angry! In this chapter, you will build an entire boss battle.

Chapter 6, *The Finishing Touches*, is exactly what it sounds like—the final gravy on this awesome mountain of 2D goodness. You'll be adding in game rounds and a start screen.

What you need for this book

This book is intentionally developed for only those who need one piece of software—Unity 4.3 or newer. That's it. Don't have Unity? No worries, you can nab a free version of this most excellent game engine from `www.Unity3D.com`.

Who this book is for

This book is written keeping anyone who wants to build 2D games in mind; however, having an existing knowledge of how to build games in the Unity game engine will be helpful. If you don't have that knowledge, no worries—we will describe things in enough detail that even those new to the engine can follow along and learn a lot. By the time you're done, you'll have an entire basic 2D platformer which you can learn from or extrapolate into something bigger and better!

Conventions

In this book, you will find a number of styles of text that distinguish between different kinds of information. Here are some examples of these styles and an explanation of their meaning.

Code words in text are shown as follows: "Import the image labeled `Platform.png`."

A block of code is set as follows:

```
case PlayerStateController.playerStates.idle:
playerAnimator.SetBool("Walking", false);
break;

case PlayerStateController.playerStates.left:
playerAnimator.SetBool("Walking", true);
break;
```

New terms and **important words** are shown in bold. Words that you see on the screen, in menus or dialog boxes for example, appear in the text like this: "To do this, select **playerSpriteSheet** in the **Project** tab and look over at the inspector."

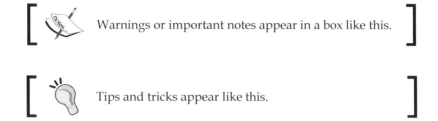

Warnings or important notes appear in a box like this.

Tips and tricks appear like this.

Reader feedback

Feedback from our readers is always welcome. Let us know what you think about this book—what you liked or may have disliked. Reader feedback is important for us to develop titles that you really get the most out of.

To send us general feedback, simply send an e-mail to feedback@packtpub.com, and mention the book title via the subject of your message.

If there is a topic that you have expertise in and you are interested in either writing or contributing to a book, see our author guide on www.packtpub.com/authors.

Customer support

Now that you are the proud owner of a Packt book, we have a number of things to help you to get the most from your purchase.

Downloading the color images of this book

We also provide you a PDF file that has color images of the screenshots/diagrams used in this book. The color images will help you better understand the changes in the output. You can download this file from https://www.packtpub.com/sites/default/files/downloads/2564OT_ColorGraphics.pdf.

Downloading the example code

You can download the example code files for all Packt books you have purchased from your account at http://www.packtpub.com. If you purchased this book elsewhere, you can visit http://www.packtpub.com/support and register to have the files e-mailed directly to you.

Errata

Although we have taken every care to ensure the accuracy of our content, mistakes do happen. If you find a mistake in one of our books—maybe a mistake in the text or the code—we would be grateful if you would report this to us. By doing so, you can save other readers from frustration and help us improve subsequent versions of this book. If you find any errata, please report them by visiting http://www.packtpub.com/submit-errata, selecting your book, clicking on the **errata submission form** link, and entering the details of your errata. Once your errata are verified, your submission will be accepted and the errata will be uploaded on our website, or added to any list of existing errata, under the Errata section of that title. Any existing errata can be viewed by selecting your title from http://www.packtpub.com/support.

Piracy

Piracy of copyright material on the Internet is an ongoing problem across all media. At Packt, we take the protection of our copyright and licenses very seriously. If you come across any illegal copies of our works, in any form, on the Internet, please provide us with the location address or website name immediately so that we can pursue a remedy.

Please contact us at copyright@packtpub.com with a link to the suspected pirated material.

We appreciate your help in protecting our authors, and our ability to bring you valuable content.

Questions

You can contact us at questions@packtpub.com if you are having a problem with any aspect of the book, and we will do our best to address it.

1
Introduction to the 2D World of Unity

In this chapter, we will dive into the two-dimensional world of Unity. We will cover the following topics:

- Introduction to Unity's native 2D support
- Sprite sheets, sprites, and sprite animations
- 2D movements

Remembering the past to build the future

Sometimes, the best way to go forwards is to go backwards. Science advances by learning how things worked in the past then improving upon them. Video games are quite the same in that they learn how things worked in the past, improve them, and then double the explosions. Although the actual improvement of games is in the eyes of the beholder, few can argue the extreme advancements that have been made in game technology—both visually and in capability.

Today, we live in a world of hyper-advanced 3D graphics rendered by computers that are powerful enough to rise against us and dominate our race. Some games even challenge the player to compare their visuals against those in real life and determine which is the game and which is real. New technological advancements now even allow a full-body scan of an actor or actress that can then be applied as a texture to a 3D model. The same model can also be built off a 3D scan of the same actor/actress and placed in a real-time game environment. The result is a 3D character that, when properly lit, can bypass the uncanny valley.

Many gamers, however, find themselves craving something a bit more classic. Some want a more approachable gaming experience without all the triple-axis complexity of three-dimensional space. Many just remember a simpler time, when a scene only traveled in a pair of dimensions rather than a full trio. It is for these gamers—who in reality make up an incredibly large group—that the art of 2D games has been revived. Many of those gamers are also people who now want to make games—and want to make the kinds of games they grew up with. You might fit that exact category! In addition, the boom of mobile devices and tablets over the past five years has also added to the resurgence of 2D gaming due to the hardware limitations on these devices. However, this revival has not come with the same dark-age technology that was used to make classic 2D games and evolved into what we make games with today. No, instead, today's 2D game technology has embraced the power that makes today's video games possible, and combines it with the design strengths that made the first video games feasible.

For this happy marriage, we combine the power of a 3D game engine with the techniques of a 2D video game to create something that is neither new nor old, yet is both.

Overkill? Most certainly not. There is actually a lot that a 3D game engine can do just as well as a 2D game engine—and much more. And in reality, most 2D game engines these days are actually 3D engines in disguise, as everything on the screen is rendered as a two-poly quad or a square built from two triangles, thanks to the power of OpenGL or DirectX.

One of today's most powerful game engines, which is affordable for large and small companies alike, is the Unity game engine available on the Web at `http://unity3D.com`. Throughout this book, we will be using the Unity game engine to learn how to build 2D video games. We will learn how to think in 2D—we will operate the camera in 2D, learn how to move in the environment in 2D, and learn how to build a platformer video game in 2D. There will even be a few surprises in there for good measure. Version 4.3 of Unity has built-in native 2D game support because they love you and your awesome game creation skills.

Before we get started, let's go over some basics. This is a professional book; however, it is written to be useful for anyone. It is expected that you will understand how to use the Unity game engine—we will not be explaining the basics, nor will we be explaining how to build games in Unity. We will, however, explain how to build a 2D game in Unity using Unity 4.3's all-new 2D capabilities. If you have been building 2D games prior to Version 4.3, then you're probably already familiar with using a number of tricks, such as the Box 2D physics engine, jointed paper doll sprites, and physics plane restrictions. All of that information is still quite worthwhile as it translates well into what Unity 4.3+ now offers.

This book uses the C# programming language for its scripting. You should have enough understanding of C# to read and understand the scripts we are supplying. We will not be discussing the basics of programming languages or why C# works the way it does (which as most programmers know, works on a mix of caffeine and fairy dust, with just the slightest hint of magic smoke).

If you don't meet those requirements, read along anyway! Since you were awesome enough to pick up this book, I'm sure you are also smart enough to learn as you go.

The first thing you will want to do now is open Unity and create a new project. On the project creation window, use the following settings: call your new project `Ragetanks` and make sure that you set the **Set up defaults for** dropdown to **2D**. This is shown in the following screenshot:

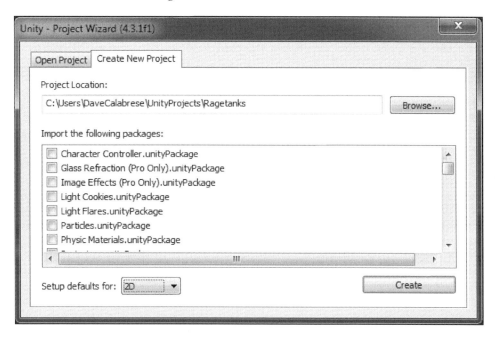

This will be the project in which our work will be done throughout the course of this book. So, grab some coffee, soda, or your favorite libation, and strap on your crash helmet. It's time to go 88 miles per hour into the future's past as we build 2D video games in Unity!

The 2D world of Unity

Unity is, of course, a 3D game engine. The first thing one must understand to build a 2D video game in Unity is how exactly to treat the engine. Sure, you may know how to treat the engine right to get a gorgeous tomb-raiding game out of it, but do you know how to make a gorgeous side-scrolling platformer? The same techniques you used for the tomb game will be used here as well; however, your way of thinking needs to be slightly adjusted.

The perspective camera

If you have ever done any work with the camera in Unity, then you may have noticed that it has two projection modes—**Perspective** and **Orthographic**. Both have their uses. And I bet you are sitting there thinking, "Orthographic. Totally. We're using that."

If that's what you said, you'd be correct! However, before Unity 4.3, it would have some drawbacks. But we aren't holding anything against you, so here's a cookie (cookie sold separately). For everyone who doesn't know the difference, it's actually quite simple. A perspective camera (on the left in the following image) is Unity's default camera. It shows the scene the way it actually is, just like our eyes see things. Orthographic (on the right in the following image), on the other hand, completely removes depth. So, no matter how far an object is from the camera, it looks like it's right there. Everything parallel remains parallel to the camera. An orthographic camera simply renders an object, or it doesn't. However, the Z order of objects is maintained. In older versions of Unity, a perspective camera would have done a great job as it would give automatic parallax support, but more about that later.

Prior to Unity 4.3, we actually would have wanted a perspective camera for the simple fact that we could make use of its depth information for easy **parallax scrolling**, or a visual effect where things further from the camera move slower (much like how they would in real life). Even in Version 4.3, if you plan to make a 2.5D game (or a 2D game that uses full 3D meshes), then you probably still want to use the perspective camera. Otherwise, for a 2D game in Unity 4.3, make sure that the camera is set to orthographic—which it should have already defaulted to by setting your project defaults to 2D.

We'll talk more about parallax scrolling and z-depth later in this book.

Getting grounded

OK, we've gone over some of the basics of the camera and models. I think it's time we started really getting our hands dirty, don't you? Here is the part where we get to start building a 2D game! Yes, it really is that easy. So, let's get started.

Pro Tip

Images for your video games, as you most likely already know, work best if they are always a power of two (2, 4, 8, 16, 32, 64, 128, 256, 512, 1024, 2048), because the video card requires image map to be a power of two. Otherwise, the image map will automatically be resized to be a power of two by the game engine. While this is not as noticeable in 3D games with mapped imageries, in a 2D game where the 1:1 art for the image map is quite important, it can easily look stretched or blurry.

Considering that this is a 2D platformer, the first thing we will want to do is build the ground. This is because without the ground, our heroes and villains would just fall through space forever.

This book comes with asset files which can be downloaded from the publisher's website. Once you acquire those assets, follow these simple steps:

1. Find the `Textures` folder, and inside that, look for the `Scenery` folder.
2. Import the image labeled `Platform.png`.
3. To keep things nice and clean, let's also create a folder called `Textures` within your project (the **Project** tab). Inside that, create another folder called `Scenery` and put the `Platform` texture in there.

Unity 4.3 now has the texture type of **Sprite**. You can find this by selecting the `Platform` texture file in the **Project** tab and looking over at the inspector. With the project in 2D defaults, it will automatically import textures in **Sprite** mode—which you can see at the top of the inspector. Most of these options will already be set properly, but let's change the texture **Max Size** to **512** and **Format** to **16 bits**. A size of 512 makes sure that Unity recognizes the image as anything up to 512 x 512 before it resizes it to something smaller. **16 bits** makes sure it's an uncompressed image which allows trillions of possible colors. That's kind of an overkill in most cases for classic 2D sprites; however, many modern sprites share similarities with modern high-resolution textures for 3D games. Unity also doesn't have a setting for 8-bit imagery, so 16-bit is a great setting to use! Compression? That tries to literally compress the image to take up less space, at the penalty of a lower quality image. In most cases, you won't want a compressed image. However, it will have its uses. Now, if you wanted your art to look more pixelated, set **Filter Mode** to **Point**. Otherwise, give **Bilinear** or **Trilinear** filtering a shot to add some excellent smoothing to the visuals.

The following screenshot shows what the import settings should look like for your sprite platform:

When creating images for a 2D game in Unity or any modern game engine, be careful not to use true gradients. You can use gradients, but the image map will need to have its format set to **Truecolor** to look proper. Otherwise, the gradient will look like a set of hard-colored segments. While the `Truecolor` property allows the image to render properly, it takes up more space in video memory.

To get this platform into your scene, simply drag the platform image from the **Project** tab and drop it into the **Scene** tab or the **Hierarchy** tab. It auto-magically appears within the scene. Make sure its position in the scene is `X: 0, Y: 0, Z: 0` and its scale is `X: 1, Y: 1, Z: 1`.

To make sure our player can walk on this, we'll need to give it some collider properties. With the platform selected in the **Hierarchy** tab, navigate your cursor to the menus at the top of the screen and then **Component | Physics 2D | Polygon Collider 2D**. You could also go to the inspector with the platform selected, click on the **Add Component** button at the bottom, and search for Polygon Collider 2D. Both ways work, and you are welcome to do as you wish anytime we ask you to add a component to an object".

With the platform selected in the **Scene** tab, you'll now see a bunch of green lines going through the platform. This is by far one of the coolest features of Unity 4.3's 2D support—it automatically creates a polygon collider based on the shape of your texture (as shown in the following image)! This saves many potential headaches. Unity determines the shape of the collider based on the alpha of your image, so do keep that in mind when creating your artwork.

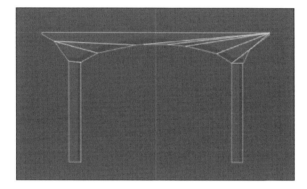

Now, in reality, we could have just used a simple box collider for this platform as well. However, we would like our enemies to be able to collide realistically with the platform. On the sides of the platform, it indents in a little. If you try applying a Box Collider 2D instead of the Polygon Collider 2D, which you can see in the following image, you'll see that it goes straight down at the sides:

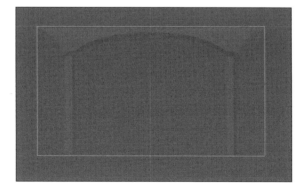

There are many platforms that a simple box collider would work properly on. However, take a look at the imagery of this platform—it has an indentation on both sides. If you were to put a simple box collider on this, the collision would go straight down from the edges of the platform. Any bullet that collided with the box collider would disappear, which wouldn't look correct. We want those bullets to disappear when they hit the actual graphics. You now have a platform!

This would also be a good time to save your scene for the first time. Name it `RageTanksScene` and place the scene within a folder called `Scenes`.

Making new friends

With our platform made, let's make a hero. Back in the assets you downloaded from the publisher's website, look for the folder labeled `Player` in the `Animations` directory. Inside the `Texture` folder in your project, create a new folder called `Player` and import the image named `playerSpriteSheet.png` to that folder.

This image is what is referred to, obviously, as a **sprite sheet**, or a **sprite atlas**. Essentially, it's just a collection of images; however, rather than each individual image taking up space in memory, all of those images only take up one image in memory. If that isn't clear, think of it like this: imagine you are hosting a holiday dinner. You could have every ingredient you are cooking within a separate fridge or every ingredient you are cooking all neatly organized in one fridge. The first option will overload your home with boxes—it is the same idea here with video memory and sprite sheets/atlases.

Say you already have a collection of sprites and need to turn them into a sprite sheet. You could build that by hand in a tool such as Photoshop; however, that gets somewhat tedious. There are some tools that can automatically build sprite sheets—check out Shoebox and Texture Packer.

So, even though we can clearly see that this image is a sprite sheet, we need to let Unity know. To do this, select **playerSpriteSheet** in the **Project** tab and look over at the inspector. Find where it says **Sprite Mode** and change it to **Multiple**. You should now see **Packing Tag**, **Pixels to Units**, and the **Sprite Editor** button. Whack that **Sprite Editor** button so we can edit the sprites.

A shiny new dialog box will open, which will allow you to tell Unity what each individual sprite is within this sprite sheet. Like most things in Unity, this is pretty easy—simply click and drag the cursor around each individual sprite. This will draw a box around each one! As you do this, a little sprite popup will be displayed in the bottom-right of the **Sprite Editor** window, which gives you some precision controls on the position of the sprite and allows you to change the pivot. You may also click on the **Trim** button to help trim the box of any unneeded empty space around the sprite, which will trim the sprite down based on the transparency of the sprite.

As you draw out the position for each sprite, you will want to make sure the pivot is set for the bottom each sprite. Another option would be to go to the **Slice** menu (top left), leave **Automatic** as the **Type** option, change the pivot to **Right,** and click on the slice button. Think of this like the origin point of the sprite—it will rotate from this point, react from this point, and exist from this point. You will also want to set the name of the sprites to something clear. Name the first 4 sprites `playerSprite_idle_01`, `playerSprite_idle_02`, `playerSprite_idle_03`, and `playerSprite_idle_04`, and the final three sprites `playerSprite_walk_01`, `playerSprite_walk_02`, and `playerSprite_walk_03`. With the sprites defined, your **Sprite Editor** window should now look something like this:

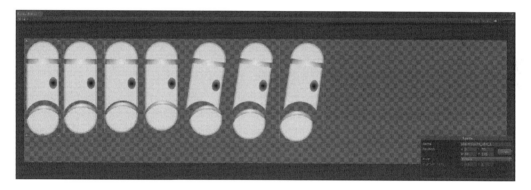

When you are happy with how the sprite setup looks, click on the **Apply** button in the top-right of the **Sprite Editor** window. You can also now close the **Sprite Editor** tab. In the **Project** tab, you'll notice that `playerSpriteSheet` now has individual sprites for each of the sprites you just set up! You now have a properly configured sprite sheet to use in the project.

Let's now place the player in the world just like we did for the platform. Drag-and-drop `playerSprite_idle_1` into the **Hierarchy** or **Scene** tab, rename the sprite to `Player` in the **Hierarchy** tab, and change the position to `X: 0, Y: 0`. The player should now be standing on top of the platform as shown in the following screenshot. If it looks a bit large, no problem—just change the scale to `X: 0.7, Y: 0.7` and it should look fine.

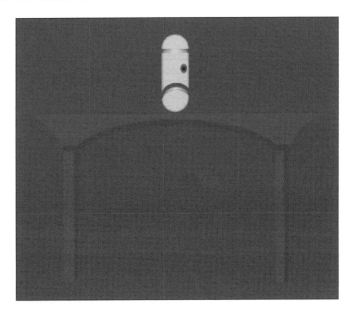

Let's move it!

With the player sprite in the world, let's set up some animations for it. From the sprite sheet, you can probably gather that our player has two animations: idle and walking. If you are at all familiar with Unity's Mecanim system, then this setup will seem familiar to you. If not, no problem—read along and we shall explain in the following steps:

1. Create a new folder in the **Project** tab called `Animations`.

2. Inside this folder, create another folder called `Player`.

3. At the top of the screen, navigate to **Window | Animation** to open the **Animation** tab. This is where we will actually build the sprite animations.

4. Select the player object in the **Hierarchy** tab then click on the little red circle (the record button) in the top-left corner of the **Animation** tab. A **Create New Animation** window will pop up.

5. Select the newly created `Animations/Player` folder, name the animation `PlayerIdleAnimation`, and click on **Save**.

You now have a blank animation, and you'll notice that a few other changes occurred as well. First off, in the `Animations/Player` folder, there is now a `Player` object along with `PlayerIdleAnimation`. This player object is actually an Animator Controller object, which Mecanim uses to know how to animate something; sort of like a description of dance steps. It is essentially a tree of animations, with certain requirements that are met to switch between different animations. We'll discuss that further in a little bit, but to keep things organized, rename the player animator object to `PlayerAnimatorController`. Now it's clear what it is.

When you click on the player object in the scene **Hierarchy** tab, you'll see that an `Animator` component has already been attached and the **Controller** field uses `PlayerAnimatorController`. This `Animator` component does all the actual animation-changing work for the sprite's animations and uses the Animator Controller fed to it as the guidelines on how to animate.

In the **Animation** tab, you'll now see that `PlayerIdleAnimation` is open. If it's not, click on the player object in the **Hierarchy** tab and `PlayerIdleAnimation` should automatically open.

Make sure the **Dope Sheet** button, which you can see circled in the following screenshot, is clicked on at the bottom of the **Animation** tab:

The next part is really easy—to build the animation. All you have to do is drag and drop each sprite into it. Start by dropping the `playerSprite_idle_1` sprite. You'll see that the sprite image appears in the dope sheet, along with a diamond above it. This diamond represents the position on the timeline that the sprite is displayed. Now add `playerSprite_idle_2` and align its diamond to be two hash lines after the first. Keep doing this until all four sprites have been added. Your `PlayerIdleAnimation` should now look like the following screenshot. If you have a lot of frames, you can also just drag them all at once by selecting them all in the **Project** tab and then dragging them over.

Clicking on the **Play** button in the **Animation** tab will now play the sprite animation on the player object; it looks pretty good, except that it snaps back to the beginning. To fix this, simply add three additional sprites to the animation after the first sprites—add `playerSprite_idle_3`, `playerSprite_idle_2`, and `playerSprite_idle_1` sequentially at the end.

What this does is it now allows the animation to play so that the robot hovers up and back down, and then the animation loops back to the beginning. Play the animation again now and it should animate just fine.

We can adjust one more item here—the **Samples** setting. This is essentially how many times the animation is sampled per second, which affects the frame rate and smoothness of the animation. Since we have already built the animation at the default value of 60 samples, we don't really have to go back and move things around; Unity will do that for us. Go ahead and set **Samples** to 125 to speed up the animation and then click on **Play**. Much smoother!

With the idle animation completed, go ahead and create the walking animation. To do this, make sure you have the player object selected in the **Hierarchy** tab, and in the **Animation** tab, click on **PlayerIdleAnimation**. As displayed in the following screenshot, this is actually a dropdown that contains the **Create New Clip** option— select that and create a new clip in `Animations/Player` called `PlayerWalkingAnimation`.

Just like before, place the sprites in the dope sheet so that the walking animation looks and plays properly. We'll let you do this one on your own for practice; however, you can use the following screenshot as a reference if you get stuck. Note that we set this animation to 80. That's because visually it animates better than 125 and is a great example of how every animation can have its own sampling rate!

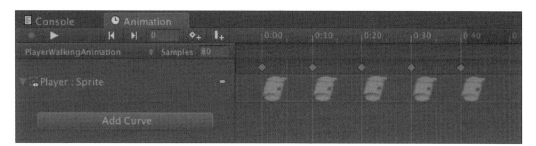

Excellent! We now have a pair of animations for our player object to use. Now, we need to set up that animator object so that Mecanim knows how to actually make use of the animations. Start by selecting the `PlayerAnimatorController` object in the `Animations/Player` folder. If you take a look at the inspector, it looks completely empty, except in the top-right corner. There's a small **Open** button. Click on it to open the **Animator Editor** tab. You should now be looking at a window that looks like the following screenshot:

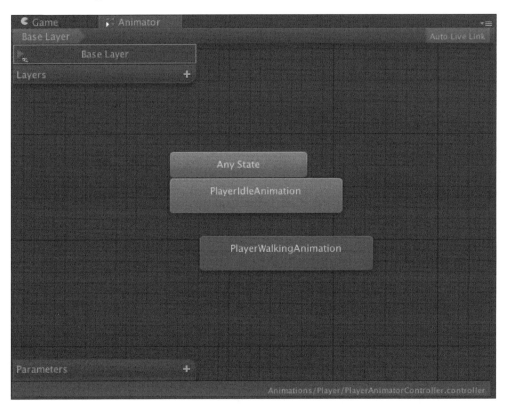

As we previously mentioned, Mecanim reads the animator trees to know how to play the animations. What we need to do here is build an animation tree. Unity was nice enough to already add both our animations to the animator for us—we just need to tell them when to play. To handle this, we will use a simple Boolean check.

At the bottom left, look for the **Parameters** window. Click on the small **+** button on that window and you will see a list of variable types. Choose **Bool** and a `New Bool` variable will be created. Name this `Walking`. To determine if Mecanim should play the idle or walking animation, we will use the `Walking` Boolean.

The orange-colored state is the default animation and the default state in the animator tree. Right-click on the orange-colored PlayerIdleAnimation node in the **Animator** tab and select **Make Transition**. This will attach the translation line to the cursor. Move your cursor over **PlayerWalkingAnimation** and click on it to drop it there. Now do the same thing, only in reverse—create a transition from PlayerWalkingAnimation to PlayerIdleAnimation. Your animator node tree should now look something like the following screenshot:

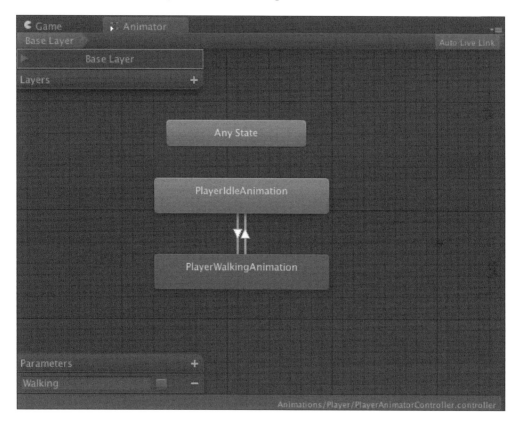

If you were to click on **Play** on the game now, you'll see that the animations play on the Player object; however, it plays the idle animation, then immediately plays the walk animation, then loops back to idle, and repeats ad nauseam. Almost there!

Let's now give those transition connects some information on how to act so that rather than playing in a loop, they actually play when we want them to. Click on **PlayerIdleAnimation**, then click on the transition, and then look over in the inspector. The transition has some simple data that it uses to know when to go to the connected animation. In this case, the animation simply waits until the time has reached 1 second, then goes to the next animation--which is why this condition is specified as **Exit Time** with the property of **1.00**. Let's change this to use our **Boolean Walking** state instead. The **Exit Time** condition is good when you wish to blend two animations; however, for the sake of this animation, it will simply play or not play; therefore, Boolean. Click on **Exit Time** to reveal it as a pop up. The **Walking** Boolean has already been listed for us; click on that. All you need to do now is make sure that the transition going into PlayerWalkingAnimation has True as the **Walking** condition, and the transition going into PlayerIdleAnimation has False as the **Walking** condition. The following screenshot shows what the animation should now look like:

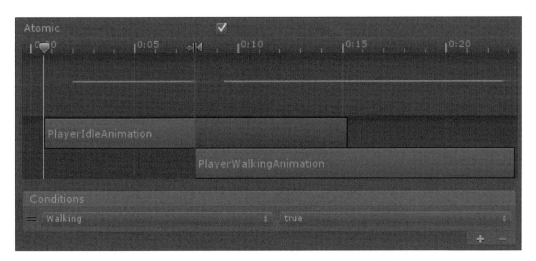

With that completed, we can go ahead and test! Perform the following steps:

1.   Hit **Play** in the game.
2.   With the game running, select the Player object.
3.   In the **Animator** tab, select the checkbox next to **Walking** under **Parameters**.

When the checkbox is active, the walking animation will play, whereas when the checkbox is inactive, the idle animation will play. It really is as simple as that.

Gotta move it!

Our player now has a basic idle animation, but we can't interact with him yet. Let's fix that. Here is where we add the ability for the player to move around the scene.

We are going to use the existing key bindings that are present by default in a Unity project. To see what these are or change them, navigate to **Edit | Project Settings | Input** and mess around. Unity stores all keybinds as axes, as they all have floating point values. This allows all input buttons for the engine to support the classic on/off function as well as support more touch-sensitive buttons and joysticks, such as those present on most modern gamepads.

Let's create a new folder in our project folder called `Scripts`, and inside that, create a new C# script. Call this script `PlayerStateController`. Here's how it should look:

```
Using Unity Engine;
Using System.Collections;
Public class PlayerStateController :MonoBehaviour
{
publicenumplayerStates
{
idle = 0,
left,
right,
jump,
landing,
falling,
kill,
resurrect
}
public delegate void playerStateHandler(PlayerStateController.
playerStatesnewState);

public static event playerStateHandleronStateChange;
voidLateUpdate ()
{
// Detect the current input of the Horizontal axis, then
// broadcast a state update for the player as needed.
// Do this on each frame to make sure the state is always
// set properly based on the current user input.
float horizontal = Input.GetAxis("Horizontal");
if(horizontal != 0f)
{
```

```
if(horizontal < 0f)
{
if(onStateChange != null) onStateChange(PlayerStateController.
playerStates.left);
}
else
{
if(onStateChange != null) onStateChange(PlayerStateController.
playerStates.right);
}
}
else
{
if(onStateChange != null) onStateChange(PlayerStateController.
playerStates.idle);
}
}
}
```

Pro Tip

If you have a game with hundreds or even thousands of objects that track events from one object, such as a player, then it would be advised to use a singleton in those cases and have the other objects keep track of the state of the player on their own. Otherwise, you can get a massive load spike if you are loading thousands of events on a level load, which would happen even if you are using a pooling system.

As you may have noticed, we listed out a number of states here. This makes up most of the states we'll use in the game. Don't worry, we'll add some more as we go on, which will show you how to add new states to the code.

This script also handles listening to the input keys. We're currently only listening to the horizontal input. If it is negative, we are moving left, and if it is positive, we are moving right. All of this is then managed by a simple Event and Delegate. This makes sure all enemies and other objects in the world can be informed of state changes to the player. All this does is open up numerous possibilities; we like possibilities.

Now, we need a script that listens to when the state changes and knows what to do when this happens. Create another script called `PlayerStateListener` and make that code look like the following code. The code is a rather large bit of code, and only part of it is displayed here. Check out the entire code in the supplied code examples!

```
// Every cycle of the engine, process the current state.
void onStateCycle()
{
switch(currentState)
{
case PlayerStateController.playerStates.idle:
break;

case PlayerStateController.playerStates.left:
transform.Translate(newVector3((playerWalkSpeed * -1.0f) * Time.
deltaTime, 0.0f, 0.0f));
break;

case PlayerStateController.playerStates.right:
transform.Translate(newVector3(playerWalkSpeed * Time.deltaTime, 0.0f,
0.0f));
break;
}
}


// onStateChange is called when we make a change to the player's state
// from anywhere within the game's code.
public void onStateChange(PlayerStateController.playerStatesnewState)
{
// If the current state and the new state are the same, abort - no
need to change to the state we're already in.

if(newState == currentState)
return;

// Check if the current state is allowed to transition into // this
state. If it's not, abort.
if(!checkForValidStatePair(newState))
return;

// Having reached here, we now know that this state change is //
allowed. So let's perform the necessary actions depending // on what
the new state is.
```

```
switch(newState)
{
case PlayerStateController.playerStates.idle:
break;

case PlayerStateController.playerStates.left:
break;

case PlayerStateController.playerStates.right:
break;
}

// And finally, assign the new state to the player object
currentState = newState;
}
// Compare the desired new state against the current, and see // if we
are allowed to change to the new state. This is a
// powerful system that ensures we only allow the actions to // occur
that we want to occur.

bool checkForValidStatePair(PlayerStateController.
playerStatesnewState)
{
bool returnVal = false;

// Compare the current against the new desired state.
switch(currentState)
{
case PlayerStateController.playerStates.idle:
// Any state can take over from idle.
returnVal = true;
break;
case PlayerStateController.playerStates.left:
// Any state can take over from the player moving // left.
returnVal = true;
break;
case PlayerStateController.playerStates.right:
// Any state can take over from the player moving // right.
returnVal = true;
break;
}
return returnVal;
}
}
```

Pro Tip

Event listeners and delegates are extraordinarily powerful. There's no longer any need to write massive amounts of state-check code for all of your objects. Say you have a huge sequence occurring in your game, such as a giant alien spaceship moving into attack position over a town. Instead of having every single object in the scene constantly check the state of the alien spaceship, just use event calls on the ship and event listeners on the reactive objects to update their local states based on the actions that occur. This saves time and headaches, giving you more time to make that sequence even better rather than spending more time just trying to make it work.

Phew! Now that the code is a bit lengthier, give it a good read and it's pretty clear what is going on. What we have here is a decently powerful **State System**. With this, we can manage how the player object acts based on other current events. Whenever the player pushes movement keys, the `onStateChange(newState);` function is called. The code then checks to make sure if the current state is allowed to transition in to the state defined in `newState`—we wouldn't want the player to start walking around when dead! If the state change is allowed to occur, then some immediate code is applied, such as changing the current animation, and then the state is set. On every `LateUpdate`, the `onStateCycle();` function is called, which allows state events per engine cycle to occur. This is paced in `LateUpdate` rather than the `Update` function to make sure the input control has been processed first by Unity.

You probably noticed we haven't added all of the states in that code yet. No worries, we'll keep adding states as needed in the coming chapters.

Apply both the `PlayerStateController` and `PlayerStateListener` scripts to the player object. Now click on **Play** and… the big moment… press the left or right keys as assigned in Unity's input setup (which default to *A* and *D* as well as the left and right arrow keys).

The player moves! You now have a walking character that the player can control!

Pro Tip

Your state system should be flexible and allow new states to be added easily. This means no state should directly rely on another state but instead can transition from one state to another. Plan your state systems in detail and in advance! Some very complex state systems go as far as having transitional states rather than just cycling states. Games have used state systems (also known as state machines) for decades, including in the original Super Mario Bros. games.

Make 'em run!

Ready for a challenge?

This is where we take a bunch of the things that were taught through this first part of the book and combine them into a culmination of events. We'll call this: CHALLENGE 1. If you just heard a thunderclap and electric guitars after reading this, it's perfectly fine—you're not alone.

When you look at the player, you may notice one very major issue. When it runs, its orientation doesn't change. The player stays facing one direction and never plays its run animation.

This is where we fix that.

Let's update the state code to change the **Boolean Walking** state of the player's animator component. Open `PlayerStateListener.cs` and access the state in `onStateChange(newState)`. Let's add the ability to play the run animation. Change the entries for `idle`, `left`, and `right` of the state code to look like the following:

```
case PlayerStateController.playerStates.idle:
playerAnimator.SetBool("Walking", false);
break;

case PlayerStateController.playerStates.left:
playerAnimator.SetBool("Walking", true);
break;

case PlayerStateController.playerStates.right:
playerAnimator.SetBool("Walking", true);
break;
```

With that one small change, you can now switch between the run and idle animations. Play the game again, and you will see the player running while moving and idling when not moving!

OK, this covers half of our current problem. Next, we need to solve that little *always faces the same direction* issue. There are quite a number of ways to solve this. The easiest, however, will be to flip the horizontal scale of the player object. Sounds crazy? Think of it this way, if you scale something from 1.0 to -1.0, it's now facing the opposite direction. This works even with us using a one-sided plane because we do not actually flip the plane to its other side—all we are doing is reversing the order in which its vertexes are rendered, causing it to render as if it were mirrored. This couldn't really get much easier, could it?

Go ahead, give it a try, and trust me, you'll like the results! Open up the same switch statement as the previous one and add some code so it now looks like the following code. Note that we are adding a new `Vector3` object at the top to grab and store the `localScale` of the object.

```
// Grab the current localScale of the object so we have
// access to it in the following code
Vector3 localScale = transform.localScale;

switch(newState)
{
casePlayerStateController.playerStates.idle:
animation.Play("idleAnimation");
break;

casePlayerStateController.playerStates.left:
// Play the Run Animation when the player is moving Left animation.
Play("runAnimation");

if(localScale.x> 0.0f)
{
localScale.x *= -1.0f;
transform.localScale  =localScale;
}
break;

casePlayerStateController.playerStates.right:
// Play the Run Animation when the player is moving // Right
animation.Play("runAnimation");

if(localScale.x< 0.0f)
{
localScale.x *= -1.0f;
transform.localScale = localScale;
}
break;
```

It really is as easy as that. Now play the game and you'll see the player object facing the correct direction while moving. You now have an animated player capable of moving left and right, updating its orientation and its animations, and doing all of this along a platform!

Summary

At this point, you have now built a very rudimentary game in Unity. While this isn't much of a game, it is the start of many possible games. Nearly any 2D platformer you can conceive can now be evolved from the point which your project is currently at. Think of it like this, you just made the primordial ooze of a 2D platformer. I salute you!

In the next chapter, we will begin with our first quest.

2
It Lives!

You've got a working game. You've got a character running around. OK, so that was cool while it lasted, but now you want to see more and do more. You've come to the right place because this is your first "Quest". Yes, quest. You're now on a quest. I suggest that you find a good chalice and a horse or, at the least, a very capable pony.

In this first quest, appropriately named "Quest 1," we will be taking our snazzy little back and forth walking game and giving it some pizzazz.

Cameras – they now stalk us!

It's one thing for the camera to see what we're doing, but it's another thing entirely for that camera to follow the player. Almost like a hungry stalker, that camera should always know what the player is doing and where they are doing it. It should also take a video of the player at all times to salivate over later, like a stalker. So, let's make that happen.

We're going to do this by creating a new script component for the camera which will be able to listen to the player's state changes. This is just one way of handling camera movements; however, for the scope of this book, it will be helpful for you if we see the power of using **events** and **delegates**, and learn a bit more about why exactly we love **state machines**.

Oh sorry! What is a state machine? Wikipedia offers a pretty nice description. However, in quick terms, a state machine (in the context of programming) is a piece of code that performs separate actions based on the current state of an object. For example, a cat has three states—awake, sleeping, and trying to take over the world. The cat's state machine would perform different actions depending on which state the cat is currently in.

Chances are that most of you already know what **lerping** is, but for anyone who doesn't—lerping is a way to smoothly transition between two values. The term lerp is actually short for linear interpolation, which is a mathematical method to fit a curve using linear polynomials. Congratulations! You are now 3 IQ points smarter.

Create a new script called CameraController and attach it to the object called **Main Camera**, which already exists in your scene. This script is going to look a little similar to the PlayerStateListener script; however, it does not need to be as complex. Make the script look like the following:

```
usingUnityEngine;
usingSystem.Collections;

publicclassCameraController : MonoBehaviour
{
    publicPlayerStateController.playerStatescurrentPlayerState
        = PlayerStateController.playerStates.idle;
    publicGameObjectplayerObject = null;
    publicfloatcameraTrackingSpeed = 0.2f;
    privateVector3lastTargetPosition = Vector3.zero;
    privateVector3currTargetPosition = Vector3.zero;
    privatefloatcurrLerpDistance = 0.0f;

    void Start()
    {
//Set the initial camera positioning to prevent any weird jerking
//around
        Vector3playerPos = playerObject.transform.position;
        Vector3cameraPos = transform.position;
        Vector3startTargPos = playerPos;

//Set the Z to the same as the camera so it does not move
        startTargPos.z = cameraPos.z;
        lastTargetPosition = startTargPos;
        currTargetPosition = startTargPos;
        currLerpDistance = 1.0f;
    }

    voidOnEnable()
    {
```

```
            PlayerStateController.onStateChange +=
                onPlayerStateChange;
        }

        voidOnDisable()
        {
            PlayerStateController.onStateChange -=
                onPlayerStateChange;
        }

    voidonPlayerStateChange(PlayerStateController.playerStatesnewState
    )
        {
            currentPlayerState = newState;
        }

        voidLateUpdate()
        {
// Update based on our current state
            onStateCycle();

// Continue moving to the current target position
            currLerpDistance += cameraTrackingSpeed;
            transform.position = Vector3.Lerp(lastTargetPosition,
                currTargetPosition, currLerpDistance);
        }

// Every cycle of the engine, process the current state
    voidonStateCycle()
        {
/*We use the player state to determine the current action that the
camera should take. Notice that in most cases we are tracking the
player - however, in the case of killing or resurrecting, we don't
want to track the player.*/

            switch(currentPlayerState)
            {
                casePlayerStateController.playerStates.idle:
                    trackPlayer();
                break;

                casePlayerStateController.playerStates.left:
                    trackPlayer();
```

```
            break;

            casePlayerStateController.playerStates.right:
                trackPlayer();
            break;
        }
    }


    voidtrackPlayer()
    {
// Get and store the current camera position, and the current
// player position, in world coordinates
        Vector3currCamPos = transform.position;
        Vector3currPlayerPos = playerObject.transform.position;

        if(currCamPos.x == currPlayerPos.x&&currCamPos.y ==
currPlayerPos.y)
        {
// Positions are the same - tell the camera not to move, then abort.
            currLerpDistance = 1f;
            lastTargetPosition = currCamPos;
            currTargetPosition = currCamPos;
            return;
        }

// Reset the travel distance for the lerp
        currLerpDistance = 0f;

// Store the current target position so we can lerp from it (have
// you explained what lerp is?)
        lastTargetPosition = currCamPos;

// Store the new target position
        currTargetPosition = currPlayerPos;

// Store the current target position so we can lerp from it (have
// you explained what lerp is?)
        currTargetPosition.z = currCamPos.z;
    }

    voidstopTrackingPlayer()
    {
```

```
// Store the current target position so we can lerp from it (have
// you explained what lerp is?)
        Vector3currCamPos = transform.position;
        currTargetPosition = currCamPos;
        lastTargetPosition = currCamPos;

// Store the current target position so we can lerp from it (have
// you explained what lerp is?)

/*Since we set the target positions to the camera's current position,
the camera will just lerp to its current spot and stop there.*/
        currLerpDistance = 1.0f;
    }
}
```

In the **Camera Controller (Script)** checkbox region in the **Main Camera** component within the **Inspector** panel, you'll find the **Player Object** field. If you haven't yet, make sure to drag the **Player** object into the **Player Object** field. This is shown in the following screenshot:

Now, save your scene by pressing *Ctrl + S* or going to **File** | **Save Scene**, and then play your game. As you move the player left and right, the camera will now move with the player, stalking the player and observing the player—creepy! As you may have already noticed, there is quite a lot of power we can now implement to the camera thanks to the use of both a state machine and events/delegates. With the previous code, not only can we track the player, but we could also implement states that allow the camera to track other objects as needed. The camera will always smoothly transition between the two objects without jumping around.

Currently, when the player reaches the ledge, they just keep going. Like a Vegas magician earning his bread, the player walks across that huge empty gap like it's nothing. It's high time we brought that player tumbling to the inky darkness below.

Falling to your doom!

The first thing that we need to do is give our player a collider. For this game, we don't need to be too concerned about the player's specific shape; so for that reason, we can use a **box collider**. We don't want to use a circle or polygon collider here because it would result in the player just sliding off the platform. A box collider gives a nice, flat surface for the physics to collide with. A box collider is also the quickest type of collider to use for performance. Select the **Player** object and attach a **Box Collider 2D** component to it, which is found under **Component | Physics 2D** in the menu bar. The collision box on your player should look like the box in the following screenshot:

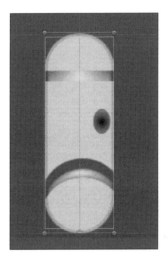

Now that the player has collision information, let's give it some actual physics. Attach a **Rigidbody 2D** component to the player. A **Rigidbody** component is sort of what it sounds like—a physical body that is completely rigid, as opposed to a **Softbody** component that would be used for things such as cloth, rubber, and hair.

With the Rigidbody 2D component attached, change its **Gravity Scale** property to 2. This scales the gravity to something a bit higher so that the player can fall in a more realistic manner. If you play with the gravity scale setting, you can see how different types of objects would have different gravity scales—it allows heavy objects to fall quickly, and very light objects to fall slowly (or even rise)!

Also, set the **Sleeping Mode** property to **Start Awake** and the **Collision Detection** property to **Continuous**. We want this to be continuous because the player is constantly moving and in control; therefore, we need the player to always be carefully checking its collisions. If you were to set it to something other than **Continuous**, there is a higher chance of the physical collisions not registering, causing the player object to pass through other colliders.

Finally, go into the **Animator** component on the player. Disable **Apply Root Motion** and enable **Animate Physics** by clicking on the checkboxes. This allows the physics to have a little more control of the animations—something we don't really take advantage of in this sample project. However, we still do this to prevent the engine from making unwanted physics adjustments.

If you play the game now, you can move the player and fall off the edges of the platform! And you can fall forever and ever, and you just keep falling—forever.

That's boring.

In the real world, you can't fall down a pit that's not more than a screen deep without turning into a shower of dead pixels (*"Shower of Dead Pixels"* just so happens to be the name of my cover band). In this game, the player should cease to exist as well. At least, they should cease to exist for a few short moments.

Falling fatally into death colliders

Like everything in this book, there are many possible ways to set up death pits and world boundaries. We are going to go over one option that allows you to specify a world that is nonrectangular and allows death pits and boundaries to exist anywhere. Let's start by adding an empty GameObject to the scene. This is going to be the core of our death trigger. In fact, let's name it that—name it `Death Trigger` as it sounds nice and ominous (and could also be a good backup name for my cover band).

Now, let's allow this `Death Trigger` GameObject to collide with the player. Add a **Box Collider 2D** component, check the **Is Trigger** checkbox, and set its **Size** to `X: 20, Y: 1`. Now, move its position to underneath the platform and set the `Death Trigger` GameObject's **Y** position to `-2.5`.

Let's add a new script. Call this one `DeathTriggerScript` and write its code as follows:

```
usingUnityEngine;
usingSystem.Collections;

publicclassDeathTriggerScript : MonoBehaviour
{
    void OnTriggerEnter2D( Collider2DcollidedObject )
    {
        collidedObject.SendMessage("hitDeathTrigger");
    }
}
```

OK! Attach that script to the `Death Trigger` object, play the game, run your player off the platform and—*nothing happens*! That was pretty anticlimactic. We promised you all kinds of player killing, yet they annoyingly continue to fall.

We need to do a few things here. First, we are going to give the player a `hitDeathTrigger` method. To do that, open up the `PlayerStateListener` script, find somewhere sanitary, and add the following code:

```
public void hitDeathTrigger()
{
    onStateChange(PlayerStateController.playerStates.kill);
}
```

Now, the player will accept the message from the trigger. However, we don't have a `Kill` state set up yet in the `PlayerStateListener` script! Let's do that. Start by scrolling to the `onStateChange` function. Inside the `switch` condition, add a case for kill:

```
case
PlayerStateController.playerStates.kill:
break;

case
PlayerStateController.playerStates.resurrect:
break;
```

Now, add the exact same thing inside the `switch` statement inside `onStateCycle`. Then, add the following code in `checkForValidStatePair`:

```
casePlayerStateController.playerStates.kill:
// The only state that can take over from kill is resurrect
if(newState == PlayerStateController.playerStates.resurrect)
    returnVal = true;
else
    returnVal = false;
break;

casePlayerStateController.playerStates.resurrect:
// The only state that can take over from resurrect is idle
if(newState == PlayerStateController.playerStates.idle)
returnVal = true;
else
    returnVal = false;
break;
```

Death and resurrection – respawning

With the state system now set up properly, we need to add some logic to the PlayerStateListener script so that it knows how to handle player death and respawn. What we want to happen is this: when the player dies, they respawn at a point in the level and the camera snaps back to this point. So, let's start by adding another empty GameObject. Name this one Player Respawn Point and set the **X** and **Y** position of it to X: 0, Y: 1.5. It should now be hovering above the same place that the player is at in the level.

This will give the game a way to find a spawn point in the level and allow us to move it around if we need to. Next, let's tell the player's state scripts to use this object. Open the PlayerStateListener script and add the following code near its beginning, where the properties are defined:

```
publicGameObjectplayerRespawnPoint = null;
```

As you may have guessed, we need to place the new respawn point object in the **Player Respawn Point** field in the **Inspector** panel. Go back to the Unity editor and add the playerRespawnPoint object to this newly created field on the Player object's PlayerStateListener component.

Scroll down a little bit in PlayerStateListener; let's modify the resurrect state inside the onStateChange method. Set the code to look like the following:

```
case PlayerStateController.playerStates.resurrect:
    transform.position = playerRespawnPoint.transform.position;
    transform.rotation = Quaternion.identity;
    rigidbody2D.velocity = Vector2.zero;
break;
```

This will now cause the player object to move to the appropriate respawn point in the scene when the resurrect state is toggled. As the camera is already tracking the player based on its states, the **Main Camera** object will automatically keep up. Currently, we don't need much else to happen except for the player to resurrect as soon as they die, so let's temporarily modify the kill and resurrect cases in the onStateCycle method to quickly jump to the next state.

```
case PlayerStateController.playerStates.kill:
onStateChange(PlayerStateController.playerStates.resurrect);
break;
case PlayerStateController.playerStates.resurrect:
onStateChange(PlayerStateController.playerStates.idle);break;
```

Now give that game a play and run off the platform. The player should now die when it hits the death trigger and then respawn wherever the player respawn point exists. Also, the camera should move as well, keeping its existing distance! Run off those platforms all you want; you're going to come back every time. See? We keep our promises.

Jump to it!

Running back and forth and falling off a platform to our death—now that is pretty cool! But you know what it isn't? JUMPING.

Jumping is going to use a number of new properties. However, most of them aren't anything that we haven't already worked with. Let's start by adjusting our states to support jumping.

Jumping for fun (and profit)

First, we need to make it so that the player object can understand how to jump. Open up the `PlayerStateController` script. We are going to add a condition to check for jumping.

In the `LateUpdate` function of `PlayerStateController`, add the following code after all of the left/right/idle checks that we have previously added:

```
float jump = Input.GetAxis("Jump");
if(jump > 0.0f)
{
if(onStateChange != null)
    onStateChange(PlayerStateController.playerStates.jump);
}
```

We put this after the left/right/idle checks so that we can find the current movement state. With this, we can determine what direction we want the player to jump in—or in other words, we are allowing the player to jump left and right as well as straight up.

OK, so now the player can be told that they are jumping. Next, let's make it actually jump! Head on over to `PlayerStateListener` and scroll on down to `onStateChange`. In the `newState` switch, add a case for jumping and make it look like the following:

```
case PlayerStateController.playerStates.jump:
    if(playerHasLanded)
    {
```

```
// Use the jumpDirection variable to specify if the player
// should be jumping left, right, or vertical
        float jumpDirection = 0.0f;
        if(currentState ==
PlayerStateController.playerStates.left)
        jumpDirection = -1.0f;
        else if(currentState ==
PlayerStateController.playerStates.right)
        jumpDirection = 1.0f;
        else
        jumpDirection = 0.0f;

        // Apply the actual jump force
        rigidbody2D.AddForce(new Vector2(jumpDirection *
playerJumpForceHorizontal, playerJumpForceVertical));

        playerHasLanded = false;
        PlayerStateController.stateDelayTimer[
(int)PlayerStateController.playerStates.jump] = 0f;
    }
break;
```

At the beginning of `PlayerStateListener`, add the following variable:

```
private bool playerHasLanded = true;
```

Under the `switch` condition `currentState`, in the `checkForValidStatePair` method, add the following code:

```
case PlayerStateController.playerStates.jump:
    // The only state that can take over from Jump is landing
    //or kill.
    if(newState == PlayerStateController.playerStates.landing
        || newState == PlayerStateController.playerStates.kill
        || newState == PlayerStateController.playerStates.firingWeapon
)
    returnVal = true;
else
    returnVal = false;
break;
```

In the `onStateCycle` method, you don't need any special code. However, to keep things clear, make sure that it has a place for jumping using the following `jump` case:

```
case PlayerStateController.playerStates.jump:
break;
```

Here, we've checked to see if the player is moving left or right and then gave the player an impulse force based on its current movement direction. The last thing we need for jumping to work is to add the adjustable variables used in the `AddForce` command. At the top of `PlayerStateListener`, add the following public variables:

```
public float playerJumpForceVertical = 500f;
public float playerJumpForceHorizontal = 250f;
```

Now, with these, you can easily and quickly adjust the values to find what seems best for you and your game.

Go ahead and play the game and press the jump button as assigned in the Input Manager for your project. By default, the jump button in Unity is always the Space bar. Your player should now jump up! You can even jump left or right while running for a running jump. Landing, on the other hand, doesn't do anything right now. Let's change that.

Wouldn't it be cool if the player did an animation while jumping? Using what you've learned about animations and changing between them, challenge yourself to add in a jump animation!

Not missing the ground

What we are going to do now is make the player register whenever they have landed on a platform. To do this, we will work with colliders that allow us to be certain not only of when we land, but also what we land on.

We could have checks that verify whether the player is moving vertically or not, and then automatically set the landing state based on the vertical movement state. However, this has a number of drawbacks including being less flexible than the method described on the following pages, and if the player slows down enough in mid-air to not be moving for a moment, the game could actually register that they landed! So instead, we will work with colliders, which allow us to be certain of when we land and what we land on; we will automatically set the landing state based on that information.

Now, let's perform the following steps:

1. Select a **Platform** object.

2. Add a new tag called `Platform` to your game by selecting **Add Tag** from the **Tag** list located in **Tags and Layers,** which you can reach through the **Project Settings** option under the **Edit** menu item, as shown in the following screenshot:

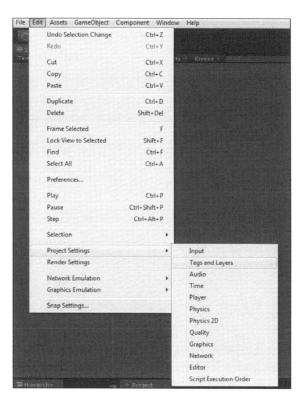

You can also access the tags and layers by selecting **Add Layer** when you select **Edit** in the **Inspector**, which you can see in the following screenshot:

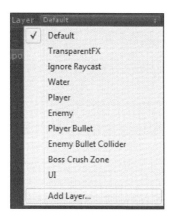

3. Set the same new **Platform** tag as the tag to the **Platform** object.

4. Create a new empty GameObject and name it `SceneryToggler`.

   On `Scenerytoggler`, add a **Box Collider 2D** component and make the **SceneryToggler** object a child of the **Player** object. The **SceneryToggler** object is going to be used for the player to know what it collided against in the scene.

5. Set the **Size** property for the **Box Collider 2D** component of **SceneryToggler** to be about `X: 0.74, Y: 0.06`.

6. With the position of `SceneryToggler` at `X:0, Y:0` and the `Center` fields as `X: 0, Y: 0.03`, the collider should be at the bottom of the player. Make sure that the collider is below and completely covers the feet area of the player, and goes below the feet area as well.

7. Also, make sure that the **Is Trigger** property in the **Box Collider 2D** section is checked.

What you should now have is a rectangular collision box that stretches out below the player object's colliders, as shown in the following screenshot. Here, you can see the big collider around the player and the new `SceneryToggler` box at the base of the player sprite:

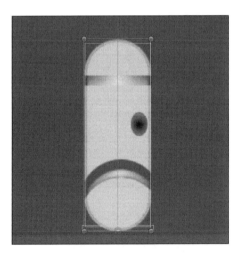

We have created a unique collider mesh. The reason we use a second Box Collider 2D component to check what we're touching below the player is because the player's box collider is smart enough to not intersect with the platform's box collider. The result is that the `OnTriggerEnter2D` of the `SceneryToggler` object will never toggle if we rely on the player's box collider—which is a good thing, because we want those collisions to be accurate!

Wait, did I collide with something?

Next, we need to set up some code so that this collider can tell the `Player` object that a specific kind of collision happened. Create a new C# script called `PlayerColliderListener`, attach it to the `SceneryToggler` object, and make it look like the following code snippet:

```
usingUnityEngine;
usingSystem.Collections;

public class PlayerColliderListener : MonoBehaviour
{
    publicPlayerStateListenertargetStateListener = null;
void OnTriggerEnter2D( Collider2D collidedObject )
    {
switch(collidedObject.tag)
        {
case "Platform":
// When the player lands on a platform, toggle the Landing state.
    targetStateListener.onStateChange(PlayerStateController.
playerStates.landing);
        break;
        }
    }
}
```

Assign the `Player` object to the **SceneryToggler** object's **Target State Listener** slot. With this, there is one issue: the state system could get into a flow where a state transition occurs, which takes the current state away from the jump even though the player is still jumping. We need to make sure the jump state is still active while the player is jumping, at least for this game. Therefore, we need to know if the player has landed or not. For that, we'll just use a simple Boolean. This will serve as our check as to whether we have or have not landed. It defaults to true because we can only jump if we have already landed.

Go back to the `jump` case in the method `onStateChange` within `PlayerStateListener` and wrap it in an `if` check with `if(playerHasLanded)`. Finally, add a case for landing in `onStateCycle`, `onStateChange`, `checkForValidStatePair`, and `checkIfAbortOnStateCondition`. Make each of those methods look like the following code snippet:

```
OnStateCycle:
casePlayerStateController.playerStates.landing:
```

```
break;

OnStateChange:
casePlayerStateController.playerStates.landing:
playerHasLanded = true;
break;

checkForValidStatePair:
casePlayerStateController.playerStates.landing:
// The only state that can take over from landing is idle, left or
right movement.
if(    newState == PlayerStateController.playerStates.left
    || newState == PlayerStateController.playerStates.right
    || newState == PlayerStateController.playerStates.idle
  )
returnVal = true;
else
returnVal = false;
break;
```

Now, the player can only jump if they have already landed, and the state system can safely transition to and from the jump state.

There is one more thing to do here. With the preceding code, we can now support the falling state of the player as well. In the `PlayerColliderListener` script, add the following function:

```
void OnTriggerExit2D( Collider2D collidedObject)
{
    switch(collidedObject.tag)
    {
        case"Platform":
// When the player leaves a platform, set the state as falling. If //
the player actually is not falling, this will get verified by //the
PlayerStateListener.
    targetStateListener.onStateChange(PlayerStateController.
playerStates.falling);
            break;
    }
}
```

Just like `OnTriggerEnter`, this will be called whenever the `SceneryToggler` object leaves another object. We then check the tag, and if this was a platform, we toggle the falling state of the player. Let's also add the falling state real quick:

- In `PlayerStateListener`, add the following `switch` case in `onStateCycle`:

```
case PlayerStateController.playerStates.falling:
break;
```

- In `PlayerStateListener`, add the following `switch` case in `onStateChange`:

```
casePlayerStateController.playerStates.falling:
break;
```

- In `PlayerStateListener`, inside the `landing` case in `checkForValidStatePair`, add the following:

```
caseplayerStateController.playerStates.landing:
// The only state that can take over from landing is idle,
//left or right movement.
if(
  newState == PlayerStateController.playerStates.left
|| newState == PlayerStateController.playerStates.right
|| newState == PlayerStateController.playerStates.idle
  )
    returnVal = true;
else
    returnVal = false;
break;
```

Got a glitch?

Now, you may have noticed a small glitch if you are holding down your jump button. The player can occasionally get stuck in the ground and then refuse to move or jump. The reason for this is how physics are checked. When objects are moving fast, often they will actually intersect another object before the collision detection occurs. This happens so fast your eyes will rarely ever actually notice it—but to the game's physics, it can mean the difference between working and... freezing in one place. We're now going to improve the capabilities of the state system to address this.

What we are going to do is add the ability for states to have a conditional check and, if certain conditions are true, abort them from occurring. We are then going to use that check to see if enough time has passed since the previous jump to allow us to jump again. This will ensure that enough time has passed for the physics of the previous landing to have finished resolving, without the player object being somewhat stuck in the ground.

Let's first add the ability for us to know how many states there are in the `playerState` enum. Open up `PlayerStateController` and change the bottom part of the `playerStates` enum to look like the following code snippet:

```
kill,
resurrect,
_stateCount // Adding this to check the state count
```

The `_stateCount` variable will now display the actual number of states in the enum. This works because the enum starts at 0. So, whatever the last entry is, provided that the last entry is not an actual state itself, it will always read the correct number of states.

Next, let's add a new line of code just below the same enum:

```
public static float[] stateDelayTimer = new
float[(int)playerStates._stateCount];
```

This array will be used to perform any timer checks on the states. Most of the states will not have timers associated with them. However, this setup allows you to easily add timers in the future if, for any reason, you have or want to do so.

> Remember that at any time you can make your code more flexible for the future; especially when it doesn't take any extra development time, *always* make it more flexible. You will thank yourself five months from now when you suddenly need to build a huge custom event into the system in a weekend to meet a deadline.

Head on over to `PlayerStateListener`, and at the beginning, add the following code to the existing `Start` method:

```
// Set up any specific starting values here
PlayerStateController.stateDelayTimer[
(int)PlayerStateController.playerStates.jump] = 1.0f;
```

Now, our jump value has an initial timer value—this will be important (as you will see shortly). Now, go into `onStateChange` in `PlayerStateListener`. In the `jump` portion of the `switch` case, change the bottom part to look like the following just after `playerHasLanded = false`:

```
PlayerStateController.stateDelayTimer[
(int)PlayerStateController.playerStates.jump] = 0f;
```

We use the fact that the timer is `0f` as part of our checks. If the timer is `0f`, then it is not running, and so we do not allow jumping. Specifically, the timer is not running while the player is in the middle of jumping or in the middle of falling, giving them all the time they need to land and start the timer again.

Having said that, you will also need to change the `falling` case statement in the same `switch` condition. Make sure that it is like the following code:

```
PlayerStateController.stateDelayTimer[ (int)PlayerStateController.
playerStates.jump] = 0f;
```

Only one more change to make in this method—we need to add the code that starts the timer backup. In the `landing` check of this same `switch` condition, add the following line of code:

```
PlayerStateController.stateDelayTimer[(int)PlayerStateController.
playerStates.jump]= Time.time + 0.1f;
```

That line will cause jumping to be allowed again 0.1 seconds after landing occurs. Once `nextAllowedJumpTime` is equal to `0f`, we can jump again.

Almost there!

Now for the meat of the code that will control this new "conditional abort" functionality—at the very bottom of `PlayerStateListener`, add the following method:

```
//checkIfAbortOnStateCondition allows us to do additional state
//verification, to see if there is any reason this state should
// not be allowed to begin.
bool checkIfAbortOnStateCondition(PlayerStateController.playerStates
newState)
{
    bool returnVal = false;
switch(newState)
    {
```

```
        case PlayerStateController.playerStates.idle:
                break;

        case PlayerStateController.playerStates.left:
                break;

        case PlayerStateController.playerStates.right:
                break;

        case PlayerStateController.playerStates.jump:
        float nextAllowedJumpTime = PlayerStateController.stateDelayTimer[
        (int)PlayerStateController.playerStates.jump ];

        if(nextAllowedJumpTime == 0.0f || nextAllowedJumpTime > Time.time)
            returnVal = true;
                break;

        case PlayerStateController.playerStates.landing:
                break;

        case PlayerStateController.playerStates.falling:
                break;

        case PlayerStateController.playerStates.kill:
                break;

        case PlayerStateController.playerStates.resurrect:
                break;
            }

    // Value of true means 'Abort'. Value of false means 'Continue'.
                returnreturnVal;
        }
```

Now, we just need to call the `checkIfAbortOnStateCondition` method when we do our state change. In `onStateChange`, just after the `newState == currentState` check, add the following code snippet:

```
    //Verify there are no special conditions that would cause this
    //state to abort
    if(checkIfAbortOnStateCondition(newState))
    return;
```

When working with a state system, it is best to include all states in any function that works with the state system. All this does is keep your code clean, and if you ever need to grow the functionality of your states, you know that the basic state call is already handled anywhere it might possibly be used.

And that's that! Jumping will no longer be locked up when you're holding down the jump key. This completes the technical functionality of jumping!

Now your player can fall off the ledge after walking off of it. And with the power of the state system, you won't be able to jump or move left or right in mid-air. Of course, if you wanted to modify things so that the player can glide left and right, the state system makes that easy to accomplish. Make it a challenge to yourself to add gliding to the player's movements!

The most astute of you, while paying attention to the console, probably noticed an error that keeps popping up: **SendMessagehitDeathTrigger has no receiver!**. What's happening here is the `SendMessage` method in the death trigger is sending messages to all colliders that hit it—which happens to include the `SceneryToggler` object. To fix this, change how the death trigger is treated. Remove `DeathTriggerScript` from the **Death Trigger** object. Then, go back into `PlayerColliderListener` and add the following case to the `switch` condition inside `OnTriggerEnter2D`:

```
case "DeathTrigger":
    // Player hit the death trigger - kill 'em!
    targetStateListener.onStateChange(PlayerStateController.
playerStates.kill);
break;
```

So what was the point of creating the death trigger in a different way before? The answer is that we could show you multiple ways to handle 2D collisions. You're welcome!

Making the world bigger

Now that your player can jump around the world, let's give them a few more platforms to jump on. First things first, let's make that platform standard. Let's create a **Prefab** with it. In the **Project** tab, create a folder called `Prefabs`. Now, drag-and-drop the **Platform** into the **Prefabs** folder to automatically turn it into a Prefab. Now you can go ahead and place more platforms around the scene by dragging and dropping the platform from the **Prefabs** folder into the scene, spacing them so the player can jump between them. This is the power of Prefabs. Because now if we need to change the platform, we simply change the one in the **Project** tab and *all* placed platforms in the game world will automatically update with the changes.

Let's keep this organized. Create a new empty GameObject and name it Platform Container. In the **Hierarchy** tab, drag-and-drop all of the platforms into this new object, making them children of it, as shown in the following screenshot:

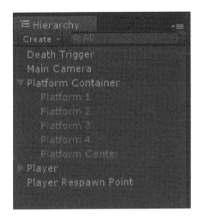

All this does is keep things a bit cleaner and easier to work with.

Let's get dangerous

Let's add one more additional feature to our jumping, walking, dying player—the ability to fire a weapon. Yup! It's time to make the player dangerous. If you feel the need to apply a lead apron and a hard hat to your person, now would be the time to do it. This is an obscure reference:

1. Dig up your downloaded assets (available at http://www.PacktPub. com/support; register to have the files e-mailed directly to you) again and import the image map titled PlayerBullet.png, which should look like the following screenshot. Use the same image import settings you've been using for all the sprites:

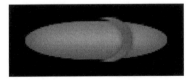

2. Drag-and-drop the PlayerBullet sprite just like you did with previous sprites into the **Hierarchy** tab.

3. Give it a **Box Collider 2D** component and check the **Is Trigger** property checkbox.

4. Also, attach a **RigidBody 2D** component and set its **Gravity Scale** to 0. Create a new tag called `Player Bullet` and set that as the tag for the **PlayerBullet** object.

Phew! OK, that was quick, but we now have a working bullet object with the base properties. One last thing to do; create a new script called `PlayerBulletController`, apply it to the **PlayerBullet** object, and make the script look like the following code:

```
using UnityEngine;
using System.Collections;

public class PlayerBulletController : MonoBehaviour
{
public GameObject playerObject = null; // Will be populated
//automatically when the bullet is created in PlayerStateListener
public float bulletSpeed = 15.0f;

public void launchBullet()
    {
// The local scale of the player object tells us which
//direction the player is looking. Rather than programming in extra
//variables to store where the player is looking, just check what
//already knows that information... the object scale!
float mainXScale = playerObject.transform.localScale.x;
Vector2 bulletForce;
if(mainXScale< 0.0f)
{
// Fire bullet left
bulletForce = new Vector2(bulletSpeed * -1.0f,0.0f);
}
else
    {
// Fire bullet right
bulletForce = new Vector2(bulletSpeed,0.0f);
}

        rigidbody2D.velocity = bulletForce;
    }
}
```

Notice that we save on extra code and variables by simply checking the horizontal scale of the Player object to determine which direction they are facing. Handy!

Now save this as a Prefab called Player Bullet and delete the current instance of it from the game world. We won't need that one.

Next, we want to add a new state to the player called firingWeapon. Open up **PlayerStateController** and add the new state to the playerStates enum. Simply add it to the end of the enum, as follows:

```
kill,
resurrect,
firingWeapon, // Our new state!
_stateCount
```

There is one minor complexity in adding this state: we want the firingWeapon state to immediately switch back to the previous state. To do this, let's add the ability to store what the previous state was.

At the beginning of PlayerStateListener, add the following line of code:

```
private PlayerStateController.playerStates previousState =
PlayerStateController.playerStates.idle;
```

Next, add support for the code to store the previous state whenever it is changed. At the bottom part of onStateChange in PlayerStateListener, modify the code so that it looks like the following:

```
//Store the current state as the previous state
previousState = currentState;
```

Finally, assign the new state to the player object:

```
currentState = newState;
```

The previous state is now properly stored when we change states—fantastic! Now we are ready to set up the code for the firingWeapon state. At the beginning of PlayerStateListener, add the following additional code:

```
public GameObject bulletPrefab = null;
```

Be sure to also add the **Player Bullet** Prefab to the Bullet Prefab slot in the Player object to fill this new property!

Next, add the proper switch / case check for the `firingWeapon` state to `onStateCycle`, `onStateChange`, `checkForValidStatePair`, and `checkIfAbortOnStateCondition`. Also, add the new state to `onStateCycle` in the script `CameraController`. We won't be using this, but it is always best to make sure all of your states in all scripts are the same, just in case you find you want to use it in the future. It's OK to leave all of the cases blank for now.

Let's add a quick transform node that we can use as the spawn point for the bullets. Create a GameObject, name it `BulletSpawnPoint`, and make it a child of the `Player` object. Assign its position `X: 0.21`, `Y: 1.08`. It should look a little something like the following screenshot:

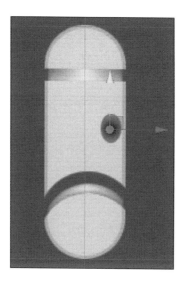

At the beginning of `PlayerStateListener`, add the following code:

```
public Transform bulletSpawnTransform;
```

Then, apply the `BulletSpawnPoint` GameObject to that new property in the **Inspector** panel.

In the `onStateChange` method's case, check in `PlayerStateListener` and add the following code to the new `firingWeapon` state:

```
// Make the bullet object
GameObject newBullet =
(GameObject)Instantiate(bulletPrefab);

// Set up the bullet's starting position
```

```
newBullet.transform.position = bulletSpawnTransform.position;

// Acquire the PlayerBulletController component on the new object
// so we can specify some data
PlayerBulletController bullCon = newBullet.GetComponent<PlayerBulletC
ontroller>();

// Set the player object
bullCon.playerObject = gameObject;

// Launch the bullet!
bullCon.launchBullet();

// With the bullet made, set the state of the player back to the
// current state
onStateChange(currentState);
```

With the preceding code, we now create the bullet, set its needed properties, and then reset the player back to the previous state, all in one shot. We also need to make sure that the checkForValidStatePair method allows this to pass. So, go ahead and add the following code inside this method in PlayerStateListener:

```
PlayerStateController.playerStates.firingWeapon:
returnVal = true;
break;
```

We also need to change a few states to allow firingWeapon to occur while they are active. So, be sure to add the following code to the state comparisons in checkForValidStatePair for the states of jump, landing, and falling:

```
|| newState == PlayerStateController.playerStates.firingWeapon
```

Finally, all we need to do now is set up the code to actually trigger all this to happen whenever the button is clicked. Open up **PlayerStateController,** and in the bottom part of LateUpdate, add the following code:

```
float firing = Input.GetAxis("Fire1");
if(firing > 0.0f)
{
if(onStateChange != null)
  onStateChange(PlayerStateController.playerStates.firingWeapon);
}
```

With that, the player can now fire its weapon! Play the game and press the `Fire1` button (by default, it's the *Ctrl* key) and then watch a consistent stream of bullets fire out from the player! However, the player currently fires a burst of bullets on every firing. So, let's add in a quick firing delay. To do this, we will simply make use of our state abort check.

In `PlayerStateListener`, add the following line of code in the `Start` method:

```
PlayerStateController.stateDelayTimer[
(int)PlayerStateController.playerStates.firingWeapon] = 1.0f;
```

Next, go into `checkIfAbortOnStateCondition` at the bottom part of `PlayerStateListener` and add the following code in the `firingWeapon` check:

```
if(PlayerStateController.stateDelayTimer[
(int)PlayerStateController.playerStates.firingWeapon] >Time.time)
returnVal = true;
```

Finally, go into the `onStateChange` method in the same script file and add the following line of code to the `firingWeapon` state in the `newState` switch condition:

```
PlayerStateController.stateDelayTimer[(int)PlayerStateController.
playerStates.firingWeapon] = Time.time + 0.25f;
```

This will cause a delay of 0.25 seconds (about a quarter of a second) between each shot. Now, bullets have a firing delay to prevent them from streaming out as fast while the player holds down the button. Also, this prevents bursts from occurring when the player just taps the firing key.

At this point, you may want to tweak the physics property of the bullet so it flies faster or differently. Try playing with the **Mass** field of the bullet's **Rigidbody 2D** component.

Bullets are better when they hit things

OK! Almost there. Let's do one more thing. Let's set the bullet to destroy itself whenever it collides with something that's different from itself, or after a preset time. Let's start by having the bullet auto-destroyed after a preset time.

Open up `PlayerBulletController` and add the following line of code at the beginning, just after the `bulletSpeed` definition:

```
private float selfDestructTimer = 0.0f;
```

Now, at the bottom part of the `launchBullet` method, let's give the timer a value with the following code:

```
selfDestructTimer = Time.time + 1.0f;
```

Finally, add an `Update` method to `PlayerBulletController` and populate it with the following code:

```
void Update()
{
if(selfDestructTimer> 0.0f)
    {
    if(selfDestructTimer<Time.time)
            Destroy(gameObject);
    }
}
```

Now when you play the game and fire bullets, they will automatically destroy themselves after 1 second.

Next, let's set up some code so that bullets will also destroy themselves whenever they collide with something. Create a new script called `DestroyOnCollision`, attach it to the **Player Bullet** Prefab, and make it look like the following code snippet:

```
usingUnityEngine;
usingSystem.Collections;

public class DestroyOnCollision : MonoBehaviour
{
void OnTriggerEnter2D(Collider2D hitObj)
{
DestroyObject(gameObject);
}
}
```

Fire the bullets now into some platforms and watch them auto-destroy.

Summary

We now have an understanding of how to create a player object with which they can interact. They can run, they can jump, and they can even collide with platforms. You know what would be really cool to have next? Some baddies. With that in mind, here's what we're going to do next in Unity 2D!

In the next chapter, we're going to create enemies, move them, attack them (ooo, scary!), and so on. We're also going to learn about particle systems for a 2D world.

3
No Longer Alone

Jumping, running, falling, dying; yeah, we got those. They rock. Now it's time to explore our violent side and beat up some bad-guys! For your second "Quest", oh warrior of Unity, it is time to add enemies. I suggest that you power up your official, licensed, awesome B-movie electricity-emitting equipment—the ones that make the cool sparks and zap noises.

Making enemies

The initial part of enemy creation is nothing you haven't already done, so let's just dive in head first and see what's at the bottom:

1. Import the `EnemySpritesheet.png` file from the assets under `Sprites\Enemy\` and then create a sprite sheet for the enemy as discussed earlier in *Chapter 1, Introduction to the 2D World of Unity*.

2. Call the first sprite `EnemyWalk_1` and the second sprite `EnemyWalk_2`.

3. Drag-and-drop the `EnemyWalk_1` sprite into the **Scene** or the **Hierarchy** tab to create the sprite in the world. If it looks a bit large to you, go ahead and change the **Scale** to `X: 41, Y: 41`.

4. Set the pivot of both sprites to be `Bottom`.

5. Create a new animation called `EnemyWalkingAnimation` and set up the frames so that they create a ping pong effect similar to the `PlayerWalkingAnimation` file (see the following screenshot for reference).

6. Rename the automatically generated animator controller named **Enemy** to `EnemyAnimatorController`, and then make sure that the `EnemyWalkingAnimation` animation is placed within it as the default animation.

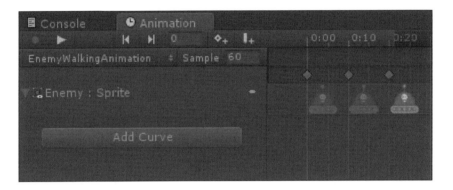

7. Make sure the **Enemy** object has a Box Collider 2D and a RigidBody 2D component.

8. On the **RigidBody 2D** component, set the **Collision Detection** property as **Continuous** and set the **Gravity Scale** to `30`. The gravity scale property is the degree to which this object is affected by gravity. In layman's terms, higher numbers will make the object heavier. The actual size and shape of the box collider on the enemy only needs to cover the center portion of the treads. Therefore, it can be quite small — just large enough to let the enemy stand on the ground.

9. Set the **Size** of the **Box Collider 2D** component to X: `1.71`, Y: `0.95` and the **Center** component to X: `0`, Y: `0.49`.

Check out the following screenshot for a reference of how that looks:

Alright! The base enemy object has now been set up. Let's start giving it some true enemy potential! Make a new script called `EnemyControllerScript`, attach it to the **Enemy** object, and make it look like the following code snippet:

```
using UnityEngine;
using System.Collections;

public class EnemyControllerScript : MonoBehaviour
{
    public void switchDirections()
    {
    }
}
```

Yup, we're starting with the basics here. These enemies are going to be easier than you think!

Make it move

For the purpose of this game, we're going to have the enemies walk back and forth on the platforms. The concept we're going to use here is that of a main object with two notification objects. The notification objects sit on either side of the **Enemy** object and simply tell it when it is about to walk off of a platform object. The notification objects do this by acting as **triggers** and checking to see when they have left the collision area of the **Platform** object:

1. Create two empty GameObjects. Name them `LeftGuide` and `RightGuide` respectively, and then make these children of the **Enemy** object.

2. Give each one a Box Collider 2D component, check the **Is Trigger** boxes on both, and set their **Size** property as `X: 0.48`, `Y: 0.64`.

3. Arrange them so that they are on either side of the enemy, outside of its main Box Collider 2D, and just off to the sides of the visual sprite. The following screenshot shows how that looks:

4. Now, create a new script called `EnemyGuideWatcher` and code it up as follows:

```
using UnityEngine;
using System.Collections;

public class EnemyGuideWatcher : MonoBehaviour
{
```

```
public EnemyControllerScriptenemyObject = null;

    void OnTriggerExit2D( Collider2D otherObj )
{
    // If this trigger just left a Platform object,
    //then the enemy is about to walk off the platform.
    //Tell the enemy that they need to switch
    //directions!
    if(otherObj.tag == "Platform")
        enemyObject.switchDirections();
}
}
```

5. Attach EnemyGuideWatcher to both the **LeftGuide** and the **RightGuide**
    objects and make sure to add the **Enemy** object to the **Enemy Object** field
    on both objects in the **Inspector** panel.

Next, we need to make sure the enemy knows how to flip its direction by reversing
its movement direction, just like we did with the player back in *Chapter 1*,
Introduction to the 2D World of Unity. Go back to EnemyControllerScript
and give it some code. Fill the script with the following code:

```
using UnityEngine;
using System.Collections;

public class EnemyControllerScript : MonoBehaviour
{
    public float walkingSpeed = 0.45f;
    private bool walkingLeft = true;

    void Start()
    {
        // Randomly default the enemy's direction
        walkingLeft = (Random.Range(0,2) == 1);
        updateVisualWalkOrientation();
    }

    void Update()
    {
// Translate the enemy's position based on the direction
// that they are currently moving.
        if(walkingLeft)
        {
            transform.Translate(new Vector3(walkingSpeed *
```

```
                    Time.deltaTime, 0.0f, 0.0f));
    }
    else
    {
        transform.Translate(new Vector3((walkingSpeed * -1.0f)
            * Time.deltaTime, 0.0f, 0.0f));
    }
}

public void switchDirections()
{
    // Swap the direction to be the opposite of whatever it
    // currently is
    walkingLeft = !walkingLeft;

    // Update the orientation of the Enemy's material to match
    //the new walking direction
    updateVisualWalkOrientation();
}

void updateVisualWalkOrientation()
{
    Vector3 localScale = transform.localScale;
    if(walkingLeft)
    {
        if(localScale.x> 0.0f)
        {
            localScale.x = localScale.x * -1.0f;
            transform.localScale  = localScale;
        }
    }
    else
    {
        if(localScale.x< 0.0f)
        {
            localScale.x = localScale.x * -1.0f;
            transform.localScale  = localScale;
        }
    }
}
```

Now you have a setup where the enemy can walk back and forth on a platform and switch directions before walking off of the ledge. With all the scripts in place, put the enemy on a platform and hit play. Now you can watch them walk back and forth! Regardless of what platform you put the enemy on, they will now walk back and forth across it.

Pro tip

With a solid knowledge of Unity's programming system, you could easily customize an enemy so that when it reaches the end of a platform, they will look for another nearby platform and then jump to it, rather than only switching directions. Try adding some additional logic and see what else you can make the enemy do!

Make it deadly

As you may have noticed, walking into the enemy currently just messes with the player's collision system. In fact, that's a little ugly; so, let's clean it up. All that we need to do here is create a **collision mask**. Start by going to the **Tags & Layers** panel of Unity, just like you did before, and add a layer for both player and enemy. Set the layer on the player to be Player and the layer on the enemy to be... you guessed it, Enemy. When you apply the layer to either object, it will ask if you want to apply to the child objects—go ahead and say **Yes**.

With the proper layers specified on the objects, we need to set the Layer Masking. Go to **Edit | Project Settings | Physics 2D** and set the checkboxes so that **Player** and **Enemy** do not collide with each other, as shown in the following screenshot:

Now when the player runs over the enemy, there will no longer be any weird hiccups in the player's or enemy's movements. With that cleaned up, let's now make the player die when it comes in contact with an enemy. For this, we are going to create another empty GameObject with a Box Collider 2D component attached. We will use another collider here so that each collider has a very specific job with very specific collision requirements. It's actually somewhat rare that the same collider can be used for multiple things simply because their positioning and sizing needs to be different. I can say from the experience of working on two entirely separate "Beat 'em up" games that each enemy usually has between three to five unique collision areas such as feet rectangle, defense rectangle, and attack rectangle..

Thankfully, Unity makes all this collision madness very simple. Name that empty GameObject `Defense Collider` and make it a child of the **Enemy** object at position X: 0, Y: 0.29. Resize the Box Collider 2D component so that it is about a quarter of the size of the whole **Enemy** object, with a **Size** of X:0.58, Y: 0.55. The idea here is that the player should be able to collide with the enemy, but if it's too precise, the game becomes far too difficult. So, give a proper defensive collision range on the enemy to allow the player some leeway to escape; refer to the following screenshot:

Let's add a new script that tells the enemy's **Defense Collider** GameObject to kill the player on touching. Wait, we already have one of those! The beauty of Unity is that it allows us to reuse scripts in surprising places. Make sure that the box collider on the **Defense Collider** object has its **Is Trigger** checkbox ticked, and then add the existing `DeathTriggerScript` to the **Defense Collider** object. Set the **Script** field in the **Inspector** panel of **Defense Collider** to `DeathTriggerScript`, and make sure that the **Layer** drop-down menu is set to **Default**.

You may remember that we just set up the enemy and player's physics layering to mask out these collisions. Just make sure that the **Defense Collider** object has a **Default** layer and it will accept collisions with the player, while the rest of the enemies continue to ignore one another—which is exactly what you want.

Now, play the game and run head-first into the enemy. What happened? The player just died and respawned at the spawn point! Yup, it really is that easy to make 2D games work in Unity.

You may notice that the message **hitDeathTrigger has no receiver!** is showing up in the console. If you do, very good, you've got your console open! The console keeps you up to date about errors, warnings, and messages—you should be watching it all the time. If you aren't watching it, now would be a great time to open it up. But how do we fix this issue? Easy; the message is showing up because now there are colliders on the player that are hitting the death trigger. Let's just tell the death trigger that we don't care if a receiver is there or not. Open up `DeathTriggerScript` and replace the `SendMessage` line with the following line of code:

```
collidedObject.SendMessage("hitDeathTrigger",SendMessageOptions.
DontRequireReceiver);
```

Play again and everything works without errors!

> **Pro tip**
>
> Learn your event listeners and delegates! It would be quite easy to make all the enemies laugh at the player whenever the player gets killed. In fact, give it a shot! Add an event and event delegate object to the player, and then add an event listener to the enemy that listens for when the player gets killed. Make the enemies laugh like the bad guys they are!

Let's go huntin'!

The enemy can now kill the player on impact. Well, that's kind of one-sided, isn't it? The player needs a way to fight back! If only the player had some kind of weapon. Oh wait, *they do*! Let's make the player's bullets actually do something. However, we aren't going to edit the bullets, we're going to edit the enemy.

The enemy's **Defense Collider** object has a perfect size and position to also act as the collider that takes damage. This is a case where a collider can have multiple purposes. Let's add a new script that is specifically meant to accept damage from the player's weapon shots. Create a new script called `TakeDamageFromPlayerBullet` and write it up as follows:

```
using UnityEngine;
using System.Collections;
```

```
public class TakeDamageFromPlayerBullet : MonoBehaviour
{
    public delegate void hitByPlayerBullet();
    public event hitByPlayerBullethitByBullet;

    void OnTriggerEnter2D( Collider2D collidedObject )
    {
        if(collidedObject.tag == "Player Bullet")
        {
            if(hitByBullet != null)
                hitByBullet();
        }
    }
}
```

Attach the script to the **Defense Collider** object inside the **Enemy** parent object. Now we can accept weapon shots from the player and call the `hitByBullet` event when it occurs. Let's modify the `EnemyControllerScript` to listen to these events.

First, at the beginning of `EnemyControllerScript`, add an object reference to `TakeDamageFromPlayerBullet` using the following line of code:

```
public TakeDamageFromPlayerBullet bulletColliderListener = null;
```

Make sure that you assign the **Defense Collider** object to this field in the **Inspector** panel. Next, add the following functions above the `Start` function in `EnemyControllerScript`:

```
void OnEnable()
{
    // Subscribe to events from the bullet collider
    bulletColliderListener.hitByBullet += hitByPlayerBullet;

}

void OnDisable()
{
    // Unsubscribe from events
    bulletColliderListener.hitByBullet -= hitByPlayerBullet;
}
```

Finally, add a function called `Destroy` to manage what happens when the enemy is hit by a bullet, as shown in the following code snippet. This code could technically go anywhere, but let's place it at the bottom of the `EnemyControllerScript`.

```
public void hitByPlayerBullet()
```

```
{
// Wait a moment to ensure we are clear, then destroy the //enemy
object.
Destroy(gameObject,0.1f);
}
```

Now, play the game and fire the player's weapon at the enemy. When the bullets hit the enemy, they will cease to exist!

You may be wondering why we used events and delegates for this when we could have just used a script component reference. Well, let me ask you this, if you did not know how events and delegates worked a page ago, do you know now? No? Well then go over it and hopefully you will get it the second time around. Essentially, each event is a type of delegate, and any object can listen to events.

Now you are ready for the future event and delegate work that we will be doing in the rest of this book, as much of that upcoming work will not work well with object references. If you don't understand, give it another read-through.

Just for fun, let's give the enemy a particle effect when they are killed. First things first, create a new **Particle System** object named `EnemyDeathFX`. As a skilled Unity ninja, it is most likely that you already know how to build these, so I won't go into the nitty-gritty of making awesome particle emitters. To help you out, we have included some particle graphics for you to use; import the graphics from the folder `Sprites\Particles`.

While I'm not going to describe how to create particles, I will, however, discuss a small requirement that you will need to fulfill to make these particles work in a 2D world. If your emitter has too much depth to it, the particles won't be in the camera view of the Orthographic camera. Keep this in mind when building out the particles, and test them frequently to ensure they look the way you want. Try and keep your emitters very, very thin. Check out the following image; that thin line in the middle is the particle system that we created. We really mean thin here.

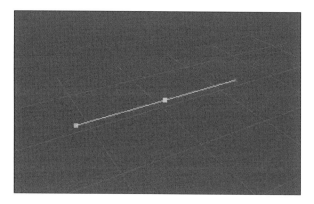

Now, build a neat-looking enemy death particle using those rules. For our enemy tanks, I will build an effect of red metal shards flying about. Store this new particle emitter as a Prefab called `EnemyDeathFX`.

In `EnemyControllerScript`, add the following code at the beginning to store the particle emitter:

```
public ParticleSystemdeathFxParticlePrefab = null;
```

At the bottom of `EnemyControllerScript`, modify `hitByPlayerBullet` to read as follows:

```
public void hitByPlayerBullet()
    {
        // Create the particle emitter object
        GameObjectdeathFxParticle =
            (GameObject)Instantiate(deathFxParticlePrefab);

        // Get the enemy position
        Vector3 enemyPos = transform.position;

        // Create a new vector that is in front of the enemy
        Vector3 particlePosition = new
            Vector3(enemyPos.x,enemyPos.y,enemyPos.z + 1.0f);

        // Reposition the particle emitter at this new position
        deathFxParticle.transform.position = particlePosition;

        Destroy(gameObject,0.1f);
    }
```

Be sure to also assign the `EnemyDeathFX` Prefab to the `deathFxParticlePrefab` property of the **Enemy** object. Now, your enemies will display a particle effect when defeated! However, the particle system we created is not getting destroyed automatically. To wrap up this task, let's make the particle system destroy itself. To do this, we will add a quick self-destruct script.

Create a new script called `SelfDestruct`, attach it to the `EnemyDeathFX` Prefab, and code it up to look like the following:

```
using UnityEngine;
using System.Collections;

public class SelfDestruct : MonoBehaviour
{
```

```
public float fuseLength = 0.1f;
private float destructTime = 0.0f;

void Start()
{
    destructTime = Time.time + fuseLength;
}

void Update()
{
    if(destructTime<Time.time)
        Destroy(gameObject);
}
}
```

Assign an appropriate value such as `1.25` to the **Fuse Length** field on the **Self Destruct** component in the **Inspector** panel, and then play the scene again. Now, you will notice that the enemy's death particle system object will clean itself up after the specified amount of time.

The swarm

At this point, your standard enemies are now complete! Save the **Enemy** object as a Prefab and create another **Enemy** object on each platform. To keep things clean, create a new empty object called `_EnemyContainer` in the **Hierarchy** tab and place all of the **Enemy** objects in there. Play the game and see how each one acts independently of the others using our events and delegates and effects.

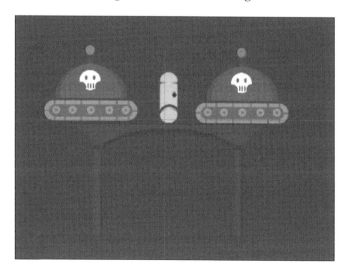

Doesn't the player just look so cozy with his new friends?

Pro tip

Tried placing two enemies on the same platform? You probably noticed that they collide with one another and prevent any further movement. Use what you have learned to modify their collision properties so that an enemy cannot collide with other enemies. Also, try to make the enemies swap directions when they are getting close to one another!

Summary

Now this is getting more fun! Running, jumping, and kicking the metallic rear of evil robots! However, wouldn't it be nice if we had more room to do all that butt-kicking? Let's do something about that in the next chapter.

In *Chapter 4*, *Give It Some Sugar*, we're going to learn about parallax scrolling, because a solid blue background is boring. We're going to kill enemies and earn points. Finally, we'll also learn about dynamic enemy generation!

4
Give It Some Sugar

Look around your world within the game. Things are happening. There are enemies. There is a bottomless pit. There are platforms you can jump between. Things are really starting to feel like a solid 2D game, all built in a 3D engine. Pretty cool, eh?

However, it is starting to feel a bit claustrophobic, isn't it? Just this one screen and a handful of enemies. Just one screen, no where to go. OK, I can't breath. The monitor is closing in on us.

Let's prevent any further hyperventilating and add more to this world. We need more room to breathe; I mean, move. You get the picture. Just breathe; we're going to get through this together. In this chapter, we're going to discuss the following topics:

* Building a bigger game world
* Parallax scrolling
* A scoring system
* Generating enemies endlessly

Expanding the world!

It's time to make the world bigger! We already have a camera that follows the player and also all the Prefabs we need to add platforms and enemies. So, let's start by building up the level a bit more. Have some fun here and put up a bunch of new platforms. Drag-and-drop the **Platform** Prefab from the **Project** tab into the **Hierarchy** tab. Make sure the player can jump between the platforms, or the game won't be much fun. Also, make sure your **Death Trigger** object covers the full area below your level. With all these new platforms, be sure to also place a bunch of new enemies on them, because awesome platforms need awesome enemies.

Next, you will want to wall in the player so that it can't leave the level area. The main concept to think of here is that you need to wall off all four sides—top, bottom, left, and right—so that the player and enemies cannot escape the level area. This is actually true for any 2D game; puzzle games need to keep their game pieces within the 2D gameplay area, platformers keep the player and enemies in the 2D gameplay area, and so forth. This doesn't need to be a box either. Many game levels for both 2D and 3D games have very odd-shaped level areas. It's all about making sure the players can't escape into the nether that exists outside the game. Go ahead and do a little something as outlined in the following steps:

1. Import the `Wall.png` image map, located in the `Assets` package in `Sprites\Scenery\Wall.png`, and set it up like the other sprites you've imported.

2. Drop one of the **Wall** sprites into your scene and give it a **Box Collider 2D** component.

3. Adjust the **Y Size** field of the box collider so that it's 20; this will make sure the player can't escape even if they jump above the wall.

4. Now go ahead and drop a **Wall** sprite on either side of your level to prevent escape!

5. Make sure the death trigger fills the entire gap below them and that the player is safely sealed inside the intended play-area.

6. Create a new GameObject called `_WallContainer` and store the `Wall` objects inside to keep things clean.

Your scene should now look something like the following screenshot. Don't worry if your enemies and platforms look different—the important thing here is that your walls surround your level on either side.

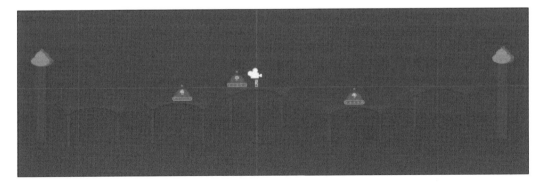

 Think you have a good sense of how the platforms are positioned in the world? Challenge yourself to build an automatic level generator!

Parallax scrolling

OK. Breathe. We're about to explain **parallax scrolling**, which is an effect where objects further in the distance move slower than objects closer to the camera. From what I understand, many of you may now need to take a moment to stop hyperventilating. Go for it, I'll wait.

As a developer, we have been asked numerous times about how to implement parallax scrolling in a 2D game. Cerulean Games, my game studio, has even had the elements of parallax scrolling as the "do or die" requirement to close a project deal with a client. In reality, this is incredibly easy to accomplish, and there are a number of ways to do this.

In *Power Rangers Samurai SMASH!* (developed by Cerulean Games for Curious Brain; you can find it in the iOS App Store), we implemented a simple check that would see what the linear velocity of the player is and then move the background objects in the opposite direction. The sprites were layered on the Z plane, and each was given a speed multiplier based on its distance from the camera. So, as the player moved to the right, all parallax scrolling objects would move to the left based on their multiplier value. That technique worked, and it fared us and our client quite well for the production of the game. This is also a common and quick way to manage parallax scrolling, and it's also pretty much how we're going to manage it in this game as well.

OK, enough talk! Have at you! Well, have at the code:

1. Create a new script called `ParallaxController` and make it look like the following code:

```
-using UnityEngine;
using System.Collections;

public class ParallaxController : MonoBehaviour
{
    public GameObject[] clouds;
    public GameObject[] nearHills;
    public GameObject[] farHills;

    public float cloudLayerSpeedModifier;
    public float nearHillLayerSpeedModifier;
    public float farHillLayerSpeedModifier;

    public Camera myCamera;
```

```
    private Vector3 lastCamPos;

    void Start()
    {
        lastCamPos = myCamera.transform.position;
    }

    void Update()
    {
        Vector3 currCamPos = myCamera.transform.position;
        float xPosDiff = lastCamPos.x - currCamPos.x;

        adjustParallaxPositionsForArray(clouds,
            cloudLayerSpeedModifier, xPosDiff);
        adjustParallaxPositionsForArray(nearHills,
            nearHillLayerSpeedModifier, xPosDiff);
        adjustParallaxPositionsForArray(farHills,
            farHillLayerSpeedModifier, xPosDiff);

        lastCamPos = myCamera.transform.position;
    }

    void adjustParallaxPositionsForArray(GameObject[]
        layerArray, float layerSpeedModifier, float xPosDiff)
    {
        for(int i = 0; i < layerArray.Length; i++)
        {
            Vector3 objPos =
                layerArray[i].transform.position;
            objPos.x += xPosDiff * layerSpeedModifier;
            layerArray[i].transform.position = objPos;
        }
    }
}
```

2. Create a new GameObject in your scene and call it `_ParallaxLayers`. This will act as the container for all the parallax layers.

3. Create three more GameObjects and call them `_CloudLayer`, `_NearHillsLayer`, and `_FarHillsLayer`, respectively.

4. Place these three objects inside the **_ParallaxLayers** object, and place the **Parallax Controller** component onto the **_ParallaxLayers** object.

Done? Good. Now we can move some sprites. Import the sprites from `Sprites\`
`ParallaxScenery`. Start placing sprites in the three layer containers you created
earlier. For the hills you want to be closer, place the sprites in the **_NearHillsLayer**
container; for the hills you want to be further away, place the sprites in **_**
FarHillsLayer; and place the clouds in the **_CloudLayer** container. The following
screenshot shows an example of what the layers will now look like in the scene:

Pro tip

Is this the absolute, most efficient way of doing parallax? Somewhat;
however, it's a bit hardcoded to only really fit the needs of this game.
Challenge yourself to extend it to be flexible and work for any scenario!

Parallax layer ordering

Wait, you say that the objects are layered in the wrong order? Your hills are all mixed
up with your platforms and your platforms are all mixed up with your hills? OK,
don't panic, we've got this.

What you need to do here is change the **Order in Layer** option for each of the
parallax sprites. You can find this property in the **Sprite Renderer** component.
Click on one of the sprites in your scene, such as one of the clouds, and you can
see it in the **Inspector** panel. Here's a screenshot to show you where to look:

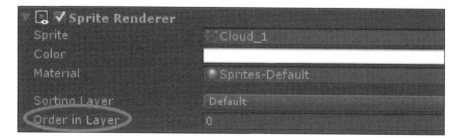

Rather than changing each sprite individually, we can easily adjust the sprites in bulk by performing the following steps:

1. Select all of your cloud layer sprites, and under their **Sprite Renderer** components, set their **Order in Layer** to 0.

2. Set the **Order in Layer** property of the _**NearHillsLayer** sprites to 1 and that of the _**FarHillsLayer** sprites to 0.

3. Select the Prefab named **Platform** and set its **Order in Layer** to 2; you should see all of your Platform sprites instantly update in the scene.

4. Set the **Order in Layer** values of the Prefabs for **Enemy** and **Player Bullet** to 2.

5. Set the sprite on the **Player** object in the scene to 2 as well.

6. Finally, set the **Wall** objects to 3 and you're good to go.

With the layers all set up, let's finish setting up the parallax layers. First, finish placing any additional parallax sprites; I'll wait. Brilliant! Now, go to the _**ParallaxLayers** object and let's play around with that **Parallax Controller** component. We're going to want to add all of those sprites to **Parallax Controller**. To make this easy, look at the top-right corner of the **Inspector** panel. See the little lock icon? Click on it. Now, regardless of what you do, the **Parallax Controller** component will not be deselected. Since it can't be deselected, you can now easily drag-and-drop all of the Cloud sprites into the Clouds array in the ParallaxController component, and all of the _**FarHillsLayer** child objects into the Far Hills array—you see where this is going.

Set the **My Camera** field to use the **Main Camera** object. Finally, let's set some values in those **Layer Speed Modifier** fields. The higher the number, the faster the object will move as the camera moves. As an example, we set the **Cloud** layer to 0.05, the **Near** layer to 0.2, and the **Far** layer to 0.1. Feel free though to play with the values and see what you like!

Go ahead and play the game. Click on the play button and watch those layers move! But, what's this? The particles that burst when an enemy is defeated render behind the sprites in the background—actually, they render behind all the sprites! To fix this, we need to tell Unity to render the particles on a layer in front of the sprites. By default, the sprites render after the particles. Let's change that.

First, we need to create a new sorting layer. These are special types of layers that tell Unity the order to render things in. Go to the **Tags & Layers** window and look out for the drop-down menu called **Sorting Layers**. Add a new layer called `ParticleLayer` on **Layer 1**, as shown in the following screenshot:

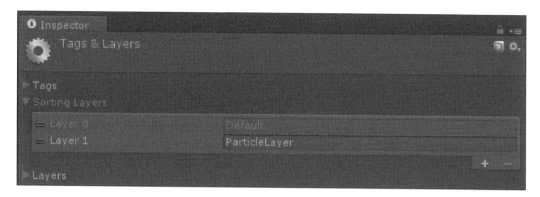

With this in place, it means anything with the **Sorting Layers** menu of **ParticleLayer** will render after the **Default** layer. Now, we need a way to assign this **Sorting Layer** to the particle system used when enemies are defeated. Create a new script called `ParticleLayering` and make it look like the following code:

```
using UnityEngine;
using System.Collections;

public class ParticleLayering : MonoBehaviour
{
    public string sortLayerString = "";

    void Start ()
    {
        particleSystem.renderer.sortingLayerName = sortLayerString;
    }
}
```

Add this script to the **EnemyDeathFX** Prefab and set the **Sort Layer String** field to `ParticleLayer`. Go ahead and play the game again now to watch those particles fly in front of the other objects.

Finally, if you want a solid color background to your scene, you don't need to worry about adding a colored plane or anything. Simply select the **Main Camera** object, and in the **Inspector** panel, look for the **Background** field in the **Camera** component. Adjust the color there as per your need. For the example game, we made this color a nice sky blue with the following values: `R: 128`, `G: 197`, `B: 232`, and `A: 0`.

The one thing you may notice we're missing is something at the bottom of the scene. Here's a nice little challenge for you. We've given you a **Lava** sprite. Now, add in a lava layer of parallax sprites in the foreground using all the info you've read in this chapter. You can do this!

Let's score!

One of the most important elements to a game is being able to track progress. A quick and simple way to do this is to implement a score system. In our case, we will have a score that increases whenever you defeat an enemy.

Now, Unity does have a built-in GUI system. However, it has some drawbacks, which will be discussed in detail in *Chapter 6, The Finishing Touches*. With this in mind, we won't be relying on Unity's built-in system. Instead, we are going to create objects and attach them to the camera, which in turn will allow us to have a 3D GUI.

Pro tip

If you want to use what this author believes is the best UI system for Unity, purchase a license for NGUI from the Unity Asset Store. I'm not the only one to think it's the best; Unity hired the NGUI developer to build the new official UI system for Unity itself.

Let's build out some GUI elements:

1. Create a **3D Text** object by navigating to the menu item **GameObject | Create Other**; name it `Score`. Make it a child of the **Main Camera** GameObject and align it such that it sits in the top-left corner of the screen.

2. Set its position to `X: -6.91`, `Y: 4.99`, `Z: 10` to get this effect.

3. Make the text color solid black and adjust the scaling so that it looks the way you want it to.

4. Set the **Anchor** field to **Upper Left** and **Alignment** to **Left**.

5. Adjust the scene to your taste, but it should look a little something like the following screenshot:

Pro tip

Unity's default 3D text font looks rather low quality in most situations. Try importing your own font and then set the font size to something much higher than you would usually need; often around 25 to 40. Then, when you place it in the world, it will look crisp and clean.

Let's make it so that the `Score` visual element can actually track the player's score. Create a new script called `ScoreWatcher` and write the following code in it:

```
using UnityEngine;
using System.Collections;
public class ScoreWatcher : MonoBehaviour
{
```

```
    public int currScore = 0;
    private TextMesh scoreMesh = null;

    void Start()
    {
        scoreMesh = gameObject.GetComponent<TextMesh>();
scoreMesh.text = "0";
    }

    void OnEnable()
    {
        EnemyControllerScript.enemyDied += addScore;
    }

    void OnDisable()
    {
        EnemyControllerScript.enemyDied -= addScore;
    }

    void addScore(int scoreToAdd)
    {
        currScore += scoreToAdd;
        scoreMesh.text = currScore.ToString();
    }
}
```

You may notice that in the preceding script, we are listening to the enemyDied event on the EnemyControllerScript. What we did here was we allowed other objects to easily create scoring events that the **Score** object can optionally listen to. There is lots of power to this!

Let's add that event and delegate to the enemy. Open up EnemyControllerScript, and in the beginning, add the following code:

```
// States to allow objects to know when an enemy dies
public delegate void enemyEventHandler(int scoreMod);
    public static event enemyEventHandler enemyDied;
```

Then, down in the hitByPlayerBullet function, add the following code just above Destroy(gameObject, 0.1f);, right around line 95:

```
// Call the EnemyDied event and give it a score of 25.
if(enemyDied != null)
    enemyDied(25);
```

Add the `ScoreWatcher` component to the **Score** object. Now, when you play the game and defeat the enemies, you can watch the score increase by 25 points each time! Yeeee-haw!

Sorry 'bout that... shootin' things for points always makes me feel a bit Texan.

Enemies – forever!

So, you defeated all your enemies and now find yourself without enemies to defeat. This gets boring fast; so, let's find a way to get more enemies to whack. To do this, we are going to create enemy spawn points in the form of nifty rotating vortexes and have them spit out enemies whenever we kill other enemies. It shall be glorious, and we'll never be without friends to give gifts—and by gifts, we mean bullets.

First things first. We need to make a cool-looking vortex. This vortex will be a stacked, animated visual FX object that is built for a 2D world. Don't worry, we've got you covered on textures, so please go through the following steps:

1. Import the ones in the assets folder under `Sprites\Vortex`.

2. Create a new GameObject called `Vortex` and add all three of the `Vortex` sprites in it, with each of their **Position** values set to `X:0`, `Y:0`, and `Z:0`.

3. Adjust their **Order in Layer** values so that the **Vortex_Back** child is set to `10`, **Vortex_Center** is set to `11`, and **Vortex_Front** is set to `12`. You should now have an object that looks something like the following screenshot:

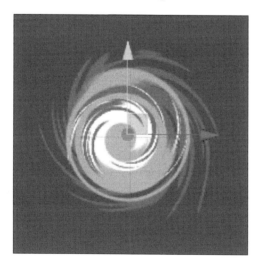

4. Go ahead and give it a nice spinning animation by rotating the **Z** axis from 0 to 356.

5. Once you're happy with it, create a new script called EnemyRespawner and code it up as shown in the following code snippet:

```
using UnityEngine;
using System.Collections;
public class EnemyRespawner : MonoBehaviour
{
    public GameObject spawnEnemy = null;
    float respawnTime = 0.0f;

    void OnEnable()
    {
        EnemyControllerScript.enemyDied += scheduleRespawn;
    }

    void OnDisable()
    {
        EnemyControllerScript.enemyDied -= scheduleRespawn;
    }

    // Note: Even though we don't need the enemyScore, we still
need to accept it because the event passes it
    void scheduleRespawn(int enemyScore)
    {
        // Randomly decide if we will respawn or not
        if(Random.Range(0,10) < 5)
            return;

        respawnTime = Time.time + 4.0f;
    }

    void Update()
    {
        if(respawnTime > 0.0f)
        {
            if(respawnTime < Time.time)
            {
```

```
            respawnTime = 0.0f;
            GameObject newEnemy = Instantiate(spawnEnemy) as
    GameObject;

            newEnemy.transform.position = transform.position;
        }
    }
  }
}
```

Now attach the preceding script to your **Vortex** object, populate the **Spawn Enemy** field with the **Enemy** Prefab, and save the **Vortex** object as a Prefab. Scatter a bunch of **Vortex** Prefabs around the level and you can get the hydra effect, where killing one enemy will create two more enemies or even more than two!

Also, if you haven't already done so, you may want to go to the **Physics Manager** option and adjust the settings so that enemies won't collide with other enemies.

One more thing—those enemies sort of glide out of their portals very awkwardly. Let's boost the gravity so they fall faster. Click on the main **Enemy** Prefab and change the **Gravity Scale** value of the **RigidBody 2D** component to 30. Now, they'll fall properly!

Pro tip

There are so many things you can do with enemy spawners that go far, far outside the context of this book. Take a shot at adding some features yourself! Here are a few ideas:

- Make the spawn vortexes play a special visual effect when an enemy is spawned
- Give vortexes a range so that they only spawn an enemy if another enemy was killed in their range
- Make vortexes move around the level
- Make vortexes have multiple purposes so that enemies can walk into one and come out another
- Have a special gold enemy worth bonus points spawn after every 100 kills
- Make an enemy that, when defeated, spawns other enemies or even collectable objects that earn the player bonus points!

Summary

So, what have we learned here today aside from the fact that shooting enemies with bullets earns you points? Well, check this out.

You now know how to build a 2D world using individual sprite objects; how to use parallax scrolling, 2D layers, and generate objects; and how to use a scoring system.

Enemies dying, enemies spawning, freakin' vortexes? I know, you're sitting there going, "Dude, OK, I'm ready to get started on my first 2D game... the next side-scrolling MMO Halo meets Candy Crush with bits of Mass Effect and a little Super Mario Bros!"

However, your revolutionary gaming exploits will have to wait a wee moment; the evil metal robots have a friend coming. This means the next chapter is going to teach you how to make the boss battle. Hike up those britches... it's going to be a wild ride!

5

The Ultimate Battle of Ultimate Destiny

The player can live. The player can die. Enemies can fight. The player can defend. Enemies can respawn.

It has been quite a journey. You have learned about 2D games in 3D worlds. You have learned the power of Unity and how to wield that power to produce 2D games.

Now we have reached the end. But to succeed, there must be one final challenge. This challenge will encompass all that you have learned, all you know, and prove that you have what it takes to save the world; or make a 2D game in Unity, which is pretty much the same thing.

The chorus sings and the guitars play. You stand there, with your weapon in hand. Everything depends on you and your abilities.

It's time for the final boss battle.

Meet the king

Boss battles in video games can be quite complex to develop. A postmortem was written on *Silent Hill 4* in the March 2005 issue of *Game Developer* magazine, where the desire to ship the game with more boss encounters was discussed. However, due to the complexity of these battles and their allotted budget, the development team had to work with what they could afford and ship games with less monstrous fear battles. If a company as massive, well-structured, and capable as Konami will fear the boss battle, then so should you.

Cerulean Games has worked on games with boss battles, and its author has personally programmed a number of these encounters. Boss battles should be looked at like a unique mini game—they will typically require a decent amount of unique code and a lot of focused testing to ensure accuracy and stability.

The first thing we should think about is what the boss battle will do, how it will challenge the player, and how it will progress. For our example game, we are going to have a rather simple boss. The king—as he shall be dubbed—will fall from the sky on to a platform, dance around allowing the player to hit him, and then jump across to fall and land on another platform. When the king has taken enough hits, he will be defeated.

Many boss battles act as a form of puzzle. In World of Warcraft, Blizzard went to great trouble to make sure their epic raid battles incorporated strategies, alternate methods, and fun events. Planning all of that in advance is key to a good boss battle. Of course, video games are iterative, so chances are you can't plan everything in advance. So, if you are going to build a very involved boss encounter, build it up in pieces. Do whatever you can to avoid a scenario where you are adding loads of features, otherwise the boss can lose its fun and you might miss your deadline!

Let's also determine what the boss should look like. Based on our evil red tanks, let's make him a big metal beast with a similar art style, as shown in the following image:

Yeah, that will work.

Open the Graphics package you downloaded from Packt's site and find the boss' sprite sheet in **Sprites\Boss** and import it to the project. Build out the sprites from the sprite sheet (like you have been doing) and animate those suckers.

We know how we want the boss battle to go down, and we know what the new challenger looks like. Now, it's time to build a boss.

Crown the king

To develop the boss battle, we are going to use everything you have learned throughout this book to assemble a single combat event in a 2D world. If you have not cracked your knuckles yet, now would be the time to do that. Always crack your knuckles before doing something awesome—it lets people know to stand back and observe the awesome event as it goes down. This is a great time to be excited. You are near the end of your production. This is the pinnacle of the game, where you have led your player to a final experience.

Place your animated boss in the scene and name it Boss. Also, add the TakeDamageFromPlayerBullet script component to the Boss object, and make sure the **Boss** object has a **Polygon Collider 2D** component.

With the collision dealt with, let's set up an event to start the boss battle. We are going to create a counter whose count increases when you kill enemies. After 10 enemies are defeated, the boss will spawn. Create a new script called BossEventController. Add the new component to the **Boss** object and code it up as shown in the following code:

```
using UnityEngine;
using System.Collections;
using System.Collections.Generic; // This is needed to support
                                  //list objects


public class BossEventController : MonoBehaviour
{
  public delegate void bossEventHandler(int scoreMod);
  public static event bossEventHandler bossDied;

  public GameObject inActiveNode = null;
  public GameObject dropToStartNode = null;
```

```
public GameObject dropFXSpawnPoint = null;
public List<GameObject> dropNodeList =
  new List<GameObject>();
public GameObject bossDeathFX = null;
public GameObject bossDropFX = null;
public TakeDamageFromPlayerBullet
  bulletColliderListener = null;

public float MovespeedmoveSpeed = 0.1f;
public float eventWaitDelay = 3f;
// Amount of time to wait between each event

public int enemiesToStartBattle = 10;

public enum bossEvents
{
  inactive = 0,
  fallingToNode,
  waitingToJump,
  waitingToFall,
  jumpingOffPlatform
}

// Current event to cycle on each Update() pass
public bossEvents currentEvent = bossEvents.inactive;
```

The boss is a bit more complex than your average run-of-the-mill red dome on treads. As a result, he will need a number of additional variables to track what's going on. The biggest ones you'll want to pay attention to here are the **event timers**, which—as you may expect—control events in the battle sequence based on engine time. The following variables are used to control the timed boss events:

```
// The node object that the boss will be
//   falling towards.
private GameObject targetNode = null;

// Amount of time to wait until jumping or
//   falling again.
private float timeForNextEvent = 0.0f;

// Target position used for when jumping off a platform.
private Vector3 targetPosition = Vector3.zero;
```

```
// Current health of the boss
public int health = 20;

// Health to start the boss at whenever the battle
  begins
private int startHealth = 20;

// Used to determine if the boss has been defeated
private bool isDead = false;

// How many enemies left to kill before the boss is
  spawned
private int enemiesLeftToKill = 0;
```

Note that in the following OnEnable and OnDisable functions, we're using all existing events. This reuse is part of their power—events can be continuously reused to check the same actions!

```
void OnEnable()
{
  bulletColliderListener.hitByBullet +=
    hitByPlayerBullet;
  EnemyControllerScript.enemyDied += enemyDied;
}

void OnDisable()
{
  bulletColliderListener.hitByBullet -=
    hitByPlayerBullet;
  EnemyControllerScript.enemyDied -= enemyDied;
}

void Start()
{
  transform.position = inActiveNode.transform.position;
  enemiesLeftToKill = enemiesToStartBattle;
}

void Update()
{
  switch(currentEvent)
  {
```

```
case bossEvents.inactive:
// Not doing anything, so nothing to do.
break;
```

You may be asking yourself, as your eyeballs roll over the following case statement, *"Yo, mister writer! Why don't we just use one of the Rigidbody 2D things and let the physics engine drop 'em? Eh?"*. The question itself though is fabulous! And I have a fabulous answer for you — physics have chaos.

So, you may think the boss is going to land in a specific position, but certain things may cause it to not happen. Maybe another object collides with it and pushes it off course. Maybe the physics causes it to not stop at the exact position you want. Essentially, this is the safest method — use movement functions to put the boss where you want it to be. If you were working on a big action-oriented game and wanted an enemy to jump a long distance — such as the Handymen in BioShock Infinite — chances are you would shut off the physics for the enemy, move it along an arc, and when it landed, turn the physics back on. Doing all this means there will never be any misses, which is exactly what the following code does:

```
case bossEvents.fallingToNode:
if(transform.position.y >
  targetNode.transform.position.y)
{
  ////// MovespeedMoveSpeed here is negative,
    so the object moves downwards
  transform.Translate(new Vector3(0f,
    -MovespeedmoveSpeed * Time.deltaTime, 0f));
  if(transform.position.y < targetNode.
    transform.position.y)
  {
    Vector3 targetPos =
      targetNode.transform.position;
    transform.position = targetPos;
  }
}
else
{
  // Create the 'Hit Ground' smoke FX
  createDropFX();

  timeForNextEvent = 0.0f;
  currentEvent = bossEvents.waitingToJump;
}
break;
case bossEvents.waitingToFall:
```

```
// Boss is waiting to fall to another node
if(timeForNextEvent == 0.0f)
{
  timeForNextEvent = Time.time + eventWaitDelay;
}

else if(timeForNextEvent < Time.time)
{
  // Need to find a new node!
  targetNode = dropNodeList
    [ Random.Range(0,dropNodeList.Count) ];

  // Set the boss position to the sky position of
    this node
  transform.position =
    getSkyPositionOfNode(targetNode);

  // Set the event state
  currentEvent = bossEvents.fallingToNode;
  timeForNextEvent = 0.0f;
}
break;

case bossEvents.waitingToJump:
// Boss is on a platform and is just waiting to
  jump off of it
if(timeForNextEvent == 0.0f)
{
  timeForNextEvent = Time.time + eventWaitDelay;
}
else if(timeForNextEvent < Time)
{
  // Build the target position based on the
    current node
  targetPosition =
    getSkyPositionOfNode(targetNode);

  // Set our event state
  currentEvent = bossEvents.jumpingOffPlatform;
    timeForNextEvent = 0.0f;

  // Also set the target node to null so we know
    to find a random one when it's time to fall
    to one again
```

```
            targetNode = null;
        }
        break;

    case bossEvents.jumpingOffPlatform:
    if(transform.position.y < targetPosition.y)
    {
        // MovespeedMoveSpeed is positive here, causing
          the object to move upwards
        transform.Translate(new Vector3(0f,
          MovespeedmoveSpeed * Time.deltaTime, 0f));

        if(transform.position.y > targetPosition.y)
          transform.position = targetPosition;
    }
    else
    {
        timeForNextEvent = 0.0f;
        currentEvent = bossEvents.waitingToFall;
    }
    break;
    }
}

public void beginBossBattle()
{
    // Set the first falling node and have the boss
      fall towards it
    targetNode = dropToStartNode;
    currentEvent = bossEvents.fallingToNode;

    // Reset various control variables used to track
      the boss battle
    timeForNextEvent = 0.0f;
    health = startHealth;
    isDead = false;
}

Vector3 getSkyPositionOfNode(GameObject node)
{
    Vector3 targetPosition =
      targetNode.transform.position;
    targetPosition.y += 9f;
```

```
      return targetPosition;
   }

   void hitByPlayerBullet()
   {
     health -= 1;

     // If the boss is out of health - kill 'em!
     if(health <= 0)
       killBoss();
   }

   void createDropFX()
   {
     GameObject dropFxParticle =
       (GameObject)Instantiate(bossDropFX);
     dropFxParticle.transform.position =
       dropFXSpawnPoint.transform.position;
   }
```

Killing any enemy, boss or regular, is a little delicate. In the case of our standard tank enemies, we just spawn a particle system and destroy the `Enemy` object. In the case of the boss, however, we want to reuse the **Boss** object. Why? So you can learn how to reuse an enemy! You're very welcome.

So, what we're going to do here is check whether the enemy is dead, and if not, generate an emitter, move the boss, and end the battle, using the following code in the `BossEventController` script:

```
   void killBoss()
   {
     if(isDead)
       return;

     isDead = true;


     GameObject deathFxParticle =
       (GameObject)Instantiate(bossDeathFX);

     // Reposition the particle emitter at the same
       position as dropFXSpawnPoint
     deathFxParticle.transform.position =
       dropFXSpawnPoint.transform.position;
```

```
    // Call the bossDied event and give it a score of
      1000.
    if(bossDied != null)
      bossDied(1000);

    transform.position = inActiveNode.transform.position;

    currentEvent = BossEventController.bossEvents
      inactive;
    timeForNextEvent = 0.0f;
    enemiesLeftToKill = enemiesToStartBattle;
  }

  void enemyDied(int enemyScore)
  {
    if(currentEvent == bossEvents.inactive)
    {
      enemiesLeftToKill -= 1;
      Debug.Log("--- Enemies left to start boss battle:
        " + enemiesLeftToKill);
      if(enemiesLeftToKill <= 0)
        beginBossBattle();
    }
  }
}
```

Now that indeed was a bit of code—lots of good stuff in there though, and lots that you should now recognize! Let's go through and review some of the important elements.

Note that at the very beginning, we create a new event for bossDied. This is exactly the same as our normal enemyDied event, which is used to track the change in scores.

This would be a perfect opportunity for you to expand on the boss battle by making use of the existing events that the enemies have. Evoke them to react when the boss dies! Make them angry! Make it so that a swarm of enemies spawn out of anger! Have fun with it because those tanks are mad!

Let's inform the `ScoreWatcher` script to pay attention to the `bossDied` event. Open up `ScoreWatcher` and add an event listener to `OnEnable`:

```
BossEventController.bossDied += addScore;
```

And, of course, be sure to unregister the event in `OnDisable`:

```
BossEventController.bossDied -= addScore;
```

Now, you can earn points whenever the boss gets killed.

Add an extra event to allow the player to earn points whenever the boss takes damage.

Next, you will notice that we use a bunch of nodes. These nodes are simple—the term node is used here to refer to anything that is locational. A node is nothing more than a GameObject that contains nothing more than a **Transform** section, as shown in the following screenshot:

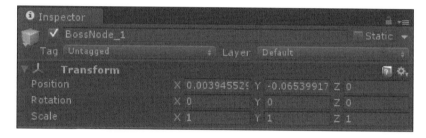

You may have noticed that anywhere we define these nodes in the code, we always define a full GameObject, and from there, we access it with `nodeGameObject.transform.position`. Well, that's not entirely needed! You may already know this, but Unity allows you to set a property in the **Inspector** panel with a component on another object! This means you could actually define the nodes as `Transform thisNode;` instead of `GameObject thisNode;`. If you challenge yourself to modify the code like this, then you can access a node's position by simply using `thisNode.position`. Handy!

For the boss, we have defined some initial nodes to be used during its initial drop at the start of the battle, which allows us to control where he goes. This doesn't do much aside from moving the boss to its initial starting point, but it could be expanded to make the boss fly around, jump about, or do whatever you desire.

Need another challenge? We just mentioned giving the boss an introduction sequence. Have a go at it!

Next, we have something new—a `List` object called `dropNodeList`. A list is essentially a container, like an array. Unlike an array though, you can use functions in a list to quickly search and see if it contains objects, add objects, pops them out, and—the best part—it's way faster than an array while working with numerous objects.

Need to know more about C# object types? Check out the Microsoft Developer Network located online at `http://msdn.microsoft.com/`. From there, you can get all sorts of resources, including information about object types! Just type something, for example, `List`, in the search box, and you'll be educated in no time.

The `dropNodeList` object allows us to define a bunch of target nodes for the boss to drop to, without needing to know how many nodes there will be. Note that to use the `List` object type, we have to add the following code at the beginning of the script file, which you should have already done:

```
using System.Collections.Generic;
```

You will now want to add these nodes to the game world. Nodes can simply be a GameObject with nothing more than a **Transform**, or if you want to be able to see them, create a sprite image just for the purpose of displaying them. Create a node for `dropToStartNode` and another for `inActiveNode`. Place the `dropToStartNode` object on the platform you want the boss to first drop towards, and place the `inActiveNode` object directly above it, only high above so that it can't be seen in normal gameplay. To make node alignment extra clear, use the boss sprite itself—then there's no question as to where the boss will land! Just be sure to add a quick component that will hide the sprite when the game begins!

The following screenshot shows how we laid out our nodes:

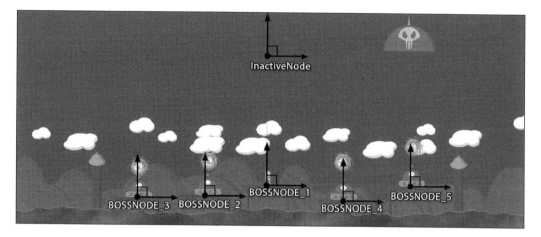

Assign those nodes to the appropriate slots in the **Inspector** panel for the **Boss** object. Create additional nodes for landing points where you want the boss to fall during his attacks, position them around the world, and add each of them to the **Boss** object's `DropNodeList`.

Dusty platforms

The boss landing on the platform is pretty cool, but it doesn't really evoke a sense of dread (or as us gamers like to call it, "oh holy biscuits what is that?!"). What would really help here is we should have a nice impact effect when the boss lands on a platform, so let's make the boss emit dust when he slams against the ground. To do this, perform the following steps:

1. Create another empty GameObject node and name it `DropFXSpawnPoint`.

2. Make the new object a child of the `Boss` object and position it near the bottom-center of the boss sprite.

3. Create a particle system that looks like dust/smoke bursting out; this will be used whenever the boss lands on a platform to give a nice visual. Use the particle image in `Sprites\Particles\Particle_Smoke.png`.

4. Make the new particle system a Prefab, and then attach this new Prefab to the **Boss Drop FX** field of the `Boss` object.

5. Add the **DropFXSpawnPoint** node to the **Drop FXSpawn Point** field.

Now, when the boss falls onto a platform, he should end up looking a little bit like the following image:

You will want to create a good particle emitter effect as well for when the boss is defeated. Add the **BossDeathFX** object to the **Boss Death FX** field in the **Inspector** panel of the **Boss** object. We've included a Prefab with the example project, which is a nice, showering explosion of red metal shards. They burst everywhere and rain down the screen for a few moments, making a very satisfying visual to defeat the boss.

Crushing defeat

We're almost done! The boss needs to be able to actually kill the player, rather than the current action where it just makes the player jiggle around a bit. In fact, when the boss drops on enemies, even they jiggle around a bit. Let's make it such that the boss crushes anything that he lands on.

The boss should only be able to kill the player and enemies by squishing them when he falls. To support this, create a new empty GameObject, call it Boss Crush Zone, and make it a child of the **Boss** object. Give it a **Box Collider 2D** component, and make it such that its size covers the bottom portion of the boss by setting its **Transform** position as X: 0, Y: -0.175, the **Size** fields to X: 3.74, Y: 0.2, and set the **Center** to X: 0, Y: 0.09. It should now be aligned at the bottom-center, as shown in the following image:

Create a new script called BossCrushTrigger, attach it to the Boss Crush Zone object, and code it up as shown in the following code:

```
using UnityEngine;
using System.Collections;

public class BossCrushTrigger : MonoBehaviour
{
  public BossEventController bossController;

  void OnTriggerEnter2D( Collider2D collidedObject )
  {
    if(bossController.currentEvent !=
      BossEventController.bossEvents.fallingToNode)
      return;

    if(collidedObject.tag == "Player")
      collidedObject.SendMessage("hitByCrusher");
  }
}
```

Note that we checked the object's tag to see whether it's the player or not. Since we now have different types of objects colliding with one another, we need a way to test these collisions. Sure, we can keep setting up collision layers, but tags can be handy too. Perhaps, you have a field of flowers, which are all the same object, but you want only one of them to be pickable. You could give that one flower a `Pickable` tag. Pretty handy, eh? So, make sure that the tag of the `Player` object is set to `Player`. The `Player` tag is added by default to a new project, so you don't have to worry about adding it.

Oh, and don't forget to populate the **Boss Controller** field on the **Boss Crush Zone** object. Next, modify `PlayerStateListener` to listen for the `hitByCrusher` message. Add the following function anywhere you want in `PlayerStateListener`:

```
public void hitByCrusher()
{
    onStateChange(PlayerStateController.playerStates.kill);
}
```

Now, whenever the boss lands on the player, the player will get killed; however, not when the boss collides with the player in other ways! As always, feel free to change and improve on the code as you desire. Note that enemies give the player points when they are defeated, but you won't want the boss crushing the enemy to earn the player points. Take a stab at working through the code to make that happen on your own. If you get stuck, take a look at what we did in the example project.

Summary

Play the game now and enjoy fighting with the enemies, taking on the boss, and repeating. The game is now a rather complete game that cycles endlessly with enemies and a boss.

Now that was a rush! A big freaking boss dropping out of the sky? Yeah, those robots were pretty upset, but your elite coding skills gave them both a defender and a way to beat that defender.

There are a few final things to do before we're done here, including some cleanup. In the next and final chapter, we'll discuss:

- Implementing game rounds with an increase in game difficulty
- Creating a basic start screen

6
The Finishing Touches

Now, this is a solid game. You've got enemies, you've got a player, and you've even got a freaking *boss*! How cool is that? I'll tell you how cool—it's wicked cool! Now only if it had a start screen and rounds that got more difficult. Oh, what the heck! I've got a few more minutes. Let's wrap up the book by adding those in. Let's add in the following:

- Game rounds
- Increasing enemy difficulty with each round
- A title screen

Game rounds

Back in the day of classic games—we're talking the times of Pac-Man and Tetris—the gameplay became more difficult with each playthrough of the game. Just like those titles of yesteryear, we should have our example game become more difficult each time you pass through it by defeating the boss. Start off by adding a new 3D Text object called Round. Place it in the upper-right corner of the screen and set it up exactly the way you did with the **Score** object, making it a child of the **Main Camera** object and everything. Also, set its **Alignment** field to **right** and its **Anchor** to **upper right** so that it will properly show on the right-hand side of the screen.

Create a new script called RoundWatcher, attach it to the **Round** object, and make it look like the following code:

```
using UnityEngine;
using System.Collections;

[RequireComponent(typeof(TextMesh))]
public class RoundWatcher : MonoBehaviour
{
```

```
public int currRound = 1;
private TextMesh roundDisplayMesh = null;

void Start ()
{
    roundDisplayMesh = gameObject.GetComponent<TextMesh>();

    currRound = 1;
    roundDisplayMesh.text = "Round: " + currRound.ToString();
}

void OnEnable()
{
    BossEventController.bossDied += increaseRound;
}

void OnDisable()
{
    BossEventController.bossDied -= increaseRound;
}

void increaseRound(int ignore)
{
    currRound += 1;
    roundDisplayMesh.text = "Round: " + currRound.ToString();
}
}
```

Now, whenever you defeat the boss, the round will increase by one. Let's use that same round number to make things more difficult for the player. In the **Text Mesh** field of the **Round** object, name its tag RoundWatcher.

If you don't remember how to set up tags, we'll remind you; they're easy! Just click on the **Tag** drop-down menu in the **Inspector** panel, add a new tag, and then go back to the object and select the tag in the drop-down menu.

Open up EnemyControllerScript and add the following code at the bottom of the Start() function:

```
// Find the round watcher object
GameObject roundWatcherObject = GameObject.FindGameObjectWithT
ag("RoundWatcher");

if (roundWatcherObject != null)
{
```

```
            RoundWatcher roundWatcherComponent = roundWatcherObject.
    GetComponent<RoundWatcher>();

            // Increase the enemy speed for each round.
            walkingSpeed = walkingSpeed * roundWatcherComponent.
    currRound;
        }
```

Make sure to also reduce the initial **Walking Speed** value of the enemy to 0.25, or else they will get crazy fast very quickly. Also, make a note that after a while, the enemies will start shooting out of the vortexes so quickly that they can actually get trapped in the scenery. Challenge yourself to adjust the code to either cap the enemy speed, make the enemies drop out of the vortexes instead of shooting out at their current speed, or come up with your own solution. That's the beauty of games such as these—the solution that you feel is right is most likely the correct one.

Give it a start screen

Finally, to wrap everything up, let's go through implementing a quick, button-based dialog. We're going to add in a start screen with a simple logo to the game as well as a start button.

As discussed earlier, using Unity's GUI system is generally not the best option due to its drawbacks, so we will be using more sprites here. There are two key problems with Unity's native GUI system. The first is performance—it is very slow compared to other solutions due to using a lot of render calls. Secondly, it is extraordinarily time consuming to build a UI with. There is no visual editor, which means you have to write everything in code; it's like HTML in the early '90s all over again. Many people, however, do swear by Unity's native GUI, but overall it's not for everyone. This is exactly why Unity is working on overhauling the entire system with a new GUI system to be added in a future update to the engine.

Let's create some containers so that we can show only what we want. Create two empty GameObjects and make them both the children of the **Main Camera** object. Name the first one `Container - HUD` and the second one `Container - Start`. Set the position of both of these GameObjects to `X: 0, Y: 0, Z: 0` to position them at the center of the camera. Move the **Round** and **Score** objects to the project **Hierarchy** tab so that they become the children of the **Container - HUD** object.

Import the `Title Screen` imagery to the project and set them up as sprites like you have done before. Place the **Title** sprite in the **Container - Start** object, give it a nice position and scale, and set the **Order in Layer** field to `100` so that it appears in front of everything else.

Now for the start button! Add another empty GameObject, name it `Start Button`, and place it inside the **Container – Start** object. Give them both an **Order in Layer** property of `100`, and make sure they are both in the exact same location with the exact same scale. Add a **Box Collider 2D** component on the **Start Button** object itself, and make sure the collider completely surrounds the button imagery inside. The **Box Collider 2D** component will actually allow the StartButtonController script, which we will write in a couple pages, to accept mouse events.

Your hierarchy should now look a little something like the following screenshot:

If you're worried that the gameplay elements—enemies and the player—could collide with the UI, then you have a very valid concern! Addressing this is easy. First, add a new layer called `UI`. Now, set all of the UI elements to the **UI** layer. Finally, adjust **Physics 2D Layer Collision Matrix** in the physics settings, just like before, to prevent collisions. After you edit the matrix, you'll have a setup that looks like the following screenshot:

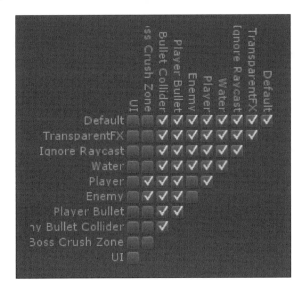

You should now have a screen that looks something like the following screenshot:

 While Unity is, at the time of this writing, working on integrating an all-new GUI system, there are some excellent GUI solutions in the asset store. For example, check out NGUI and Scaleform.

Now you've got a basic title screen set up. Let's add in some basics so that we can control which UI containers are displayed. Add a new script called GameStates, attach it to the **Main Camera**, and make it look like the following script. You could technically add the GameStates script to any object—the camera is just a nice, existing central object.

```
using UnityEngine;
using System.Collections;
```

```
public class GameStates : MonoBehaviour
{
    public GameObject hudContainer;
    public GameObject titleContainer;
    public static bool gameActive = false;

    public enum displayStates
    {
        titleScreen = 0,
        hudScreen
    }

    void Start()
    {
        changeDisplayState(displayStates.titleScreen);
    }

    public void changeDisplayState(displayStates newState)
    {
        hudContainer.SetActive(false);
        titleContainer.SetActive(false);

        switch(newState)
        {
            case displayStates.titleScreen:
                gameActive = false;
                titleContainer.SetActive(true);
            break;

            case displayStates.hudScreen:
                gameActive = true;
                hudContainer.SetActive(true);
            break;
        }
    }

    public void startGame()
    {
        changeDisplayState(displayStates.hudScreen);
    }
}
```

The last thing you will need is a way to interface with the **START!** button. Create one final script called `StartButtonController` and code it as shown in the following script:

```
using UnityEngine;
using System.Collections;

public class StartButtonController : MonoBehaviour
{
    public GameObject upSprite;
    public GameObject downSprite;
    public float downTime = 0.1f;
    public GameStates stateManager = null;

    private enum buttonStates
    {
        up = 0,
        down
    }

    private buttonStates currentState = buttonStates.up;
    private float nextStateTime = 0.0f;

    void Start()
    {
        upSprite.SetActive(true);
        downSprite.SetActive(false);
    }

    void OnMouseDown()
    {
        if(nextStateTime == 0.0f && currentState ==
StartButtonController.buttonStates.up)
        {
            nextStateTime = Time.time + downTime;
            upSprite.SetActive(false);
            downSprite.SetActive(true);
            currentState = StartButtonController.buttonStates.down;
        }
    }

    void Update()
```

```
        {
            if(nextStateTime > 0.0f)
            {
                if(nextStateTime < Time.time)
                {
                    // Set the button back to its 'up' state
                    nextStateTime = 0.0f;
                    upSprite.SetActive(true);
                    downSprite.SetActive(false);
                    currentState = StartButtonController.buttonStates.up;

                    // Start the game!
                    stateManager.startGame();
                }
            }
        }
    }
```

Now that you've added `StartButtonController` to the start button, populate its various fields and you can try it out! Now when you start the game, it will launch on the title screen, and when you click on the **START!** button, it will go to the gameplay we have seen this whole time.

Once you play the game, you will probably notice the one final thing we need to clean up. The player is able to move on the title screen. Let's use that global `GameStates.gameActive` Boolean field to fix that.

Let's fix the player movement first. Open `PlayerStateController`, and at the beginning of `LateUpdate()`, add the following code:

```
if(!GameStates.gameActive)
    return;
```

Now the game won't accept any input unless it is actually active. Other ways to accomplish this include setting the timescale of the engine to 0 when the game isn't running, or only generating the player and enemies after the game starts. Also, if you haven't done so already, remove the enemy from the center platform. We don't need him to be on top of the player as soon as the game starts!

Pro tip

Using sprites or 3D models for our GUIs gives us the added benefit of having animated elements. Try your hand at making the buttons scale, the UI slide in and out of the screen, and in general, just have fun with Unity's animation tool to create awesome GUI animations!

Summary

In this final chapter, you learned how to set up game rounds that affected the gameplay and build out a simple menu screen.

It has been quite a journey. At this point, you should have a very good feeling for what it takes to build a 2D game in the Unity game engine. Overall, it is a rather simple transition from 3D to 2D games, provided you follow the guidelines listed in this book.

In reality, much of what was discussed here are raw examples, and they can be greatly improved, merged, or generally molded to be more of what your game needs. There is so much that could be expanded upon to turn *RageTanks* into a true platformer with more levels, more bosses, more enemies, and even multiple characters. And with the power of Unity and the techniques described in this book, this would be quite easy to do.

So, diligent reader, where should you go from here? Why don't you try expanding *RageTanks* on your own! Here are some things you can try:

- Give the player health and a visual health bar, and make it lose health with each touch of an enemy rather than simply dying

- Add in health pickups for the player to collect

- Make the enemies capable of firing weapons at the player when the player is nearby

- Give the boss improved AI so that he will try and land on the player

- In the boss battle, give the player a fighting chance; add a warning arrow to the platform that the boss will land on

Pro tip

Take your Unity game development to an entirely new plane of reality. Pick up other Unity books from Packt Publishing to understand the engine from every possible angle, allowing your capabilities to be nothing short of godly.

Thank you, dear reader, for taking the time to read this book. It has been a pleasure writing it, and I hope you have had just as much fun reading it as I did writing. Most importantly, I hope you have learned quite a lot from this book and are now much more comfortable in producing 2D games in the Unity game engine!

Until the next book, this is your friendly neighborhood Dave Calabrese, signing off.

Index

Unity 3.x Scripting

ISBN: 978-1-84969-230-4   Paperback: 292 pages

Write effcient, reusable scripts to build custom characters, game environments, and control enemy AI in your Unity game

1. Make your characters interact with buttons and program-triggered action sequences.

2. Create custom characters and code dynamic objects and players' interaction with them.

3. Synchronize movement of character and environmental objects.

4. Add and control animations to new and existing characters.

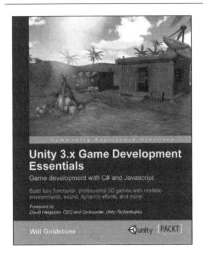

Unity 3.x Game Development Essentials

ISBN: 978-1-84969-144-4   Paperback: 488 pages

Build fully functional, professional 3D games with realistic environments, sound, dynamic effects, and more!

1. Kick start your game development, and build ready-to-play 3D games with ease.

2. Understand key concepts in game design including scripting, physics, instantiation, particle effects, and more.

3. Test & optimize your game to perfection with essential tips-and-tricks.

Please check **www.PacktPub.com** for information on our titles

PUBLISHING

Unity 3D Game Development
by Example

A seat-of-your-pants manual for building fun,
groovy little games quickly

Beginner's Guide

Ryan Henson Creighton

Unity 3D Game Development by Example Beginner's Guide

ISBN: 978-1-84969-054-6   Paperback: 384 pages

A seat-of-your-pants manual for building fun,
groovy little games quickly

1. Build fun games using the free Unity 3D game
   engine even if you've never coded before.

2. Learn how to "skin" projects to make totally
   different games from the same file – more
   games, less effort!

3. Deploy your games to the Internet so that your
   friends and family can play them.

4. Packed with ideas, inspiration, and advice for
   your own game design and development.

Unity iOS Essentials

Develop high performance, fun iOS games using
Unity 3D

Robert Wiebe   PACKT

Unity iOS Essentials

ISBN: 978-1-84969-182-6   Paperback: 358 pages

Develop high performance, fun iOS games using
Unity 3D

1. Learn key strategies and follow practical
   guidelines for creating Unity 3D games for
   iOS devices.

2. Learn how to plan your game levels to optimize
   performance on iOS devices using advanced
   game concepts.

3. Full of tips, scripts, shaders, and complete
   Unity 3D projects to guide you through game
   creation on iOS from start to finish.

Please check **www.PacktPub.com** for information on our titles

9567909R00073

Made in the USA
San Bernardino, CA
19 March 2014